stress and how to avoid it

stress and how to avoid it

Dr Tom Stuttaford

Little Books by Big Names™

First published in the United Kingdom in 2004 by Little Books Ltd,
48 Catherine Place, London SW1E 6HL

10 9 8 7 6 5 4 3 2 1

A CIP catalogue record for this book is available from the British Library.

ISBN: 1 904435 09 2

My thanks to:
Jamie Ambrose, editor extraordinaire, who has completed with an impossible
schedule when producing this book and has won through against all the odds
without ever becoming irritable and showing the stress she must have been
feeling; thanks to Marcella Edwards for her help at a crucial moment, and to
my colleague Rebecca Wallersteiner, whose life has been made even more
stressful by its writing. Thanks are always owed to Pam, my wife, and the rest
of the family, who have had to put up with me muttering away in the small
hours as I read the latest proofs. Thanks also to the design team, Ian Hughes,
Debbie Clement and Gray Jolliffe, the cartoonist, as well as to
the printers, Bookmarque, for their efficiency.

Printed and bound in Great Britain by Bookmarque Ltd, Croydon

Contents

Introduction

The twenty-first century is an age of tensions, anxiety and the stress that stems from them. Employment no longer provides a job for life and a career with an obvious beginning, middle and end. The concept that an organization exchanges consideration and care in return for loyalty and conscientious work has gone. Home life, too, is under siege, undermined by long hours at work, lengthy commutes and two working parents. It is under siege from the complexity and yet homogenization of modern living.

With problems existing both at work and at home, few people today are free of stress. Everyone has a breaking point; the only question is at what stage the break will occur. Nobody is too strong not to be affected, so that even those who continue apparently unscathed are also suffering from stress-related diseases such as high blood pressure, heart attacks and strokes as well as the emotional and psychological distress caused by everyday pressures.

Before any disease can be successfully treated, its cause has to be understood. Typhoid and cholera would still be endemic if public-health doctors hadn't realized that epidemics of both were related to contaminated water supplies – hence nineteenth-century doctors were rightly obsessed by the diseases that stemmed from lack of sanitation. Twentieth-century doctors defeated many of the other common infections, including measles, whooping cough, dyphtheria and polio, by producing immunization programmes.

In the twenty-first century, the pressures on the human body are different. People are now beset by the adverse effects of an over-civilized, over-competitive and overcrowded world. The life of the ordinary person today isn't leisurely. There isn't time to stand and stare, nor is there the opportunity to dawdle. To be successful, people have to hurry, and in hurrying there is a danger that they will lose all the enjoyment of life.

The object of this book is to analyze those factors and to draw attention to those that create the stress of modern life. People now have to be their own doctors in the battle against the diseases of stress. They have to understand its causes, so that they may alter their lifestyles to enable them to live longer, and to enjoy themselves more while living those extra years.

When dealing with any disease, the first objective must be to avoid it. It is hoped that this book will help you to avoid the difficulties that trouble others. It may even prevent you from laying up trouble ahead to plague you in the future. We, the doctors, can add a few tips that may form the basis of ideas for your future, but altering your overall lifestyle is something you will have to plan.

The other aim is to enjoy life as well as to live longer. It is impossible to teach people how to enjoy themselves and how to have fun – what is pleasurable for one person may be another's idea of hell. *Stress and How to Avoid It* isn't, therefore, a book of recipes for never-ending jollity and happiness, but it is intended to point out some of the hazards in life's journey. Falling into these pitfalls may cause such tensions that the ensuing stress removes the enjoyment from any extra-curricular activity, whether it is fly-fishing, following your local team or shopping.

Many people who read this book will have been born with genes that have given them personalities which make them vulnerable to stress. There are few people so vulnerable that they cannot alter a lifestyle in small ways to make it more stress-resistant. Even if only one person who reads this book has a better and less stressful life as a result, it will have been worth writing.

1

Stress and personality types

Many books have been written on the desirability of avoiding stress – as if stress were an option as easily taken as deciding to go to the gym or to enjoy a round of golf. The first step towards reducing the ill effects of stress is to understand the characters of the people who suffer from it. Over the years, psychologists have divided people into two main stress categories: Types A and B. Simplistic as this classification is, it works for the most part. Most people, of course, are a mixture, and in a bid to better define character types, two additional categories, C and T, have been devised.

Type A personalities

Some people are born ambitious, intelligent worriers, possibly with the added spur of competitive parents; individuals with this background and these attributes are never going to become passive, laid-back meditators. Furthermore, when they are ready to marry, any advice about choosing a partner who is bright but easy-going and relaxed – in order to produce a less driven atmosphere when they start their own home – will fall on deaf ears. Competitive men and women are attracted by high-powered, ambitious people who are as likely to be as stressed as their suitors; thus, the cycle will probably continue from generation to generation. This is the classic example of a Type A personality, and it is these individuals who are most likely to suffer stress.

People with a Type A personality are never still, and they are intent on succeeding. They are ambitious, goal-orientated and impatient; even their speech and eating are hurried. They do several things at once. It has been said that the classic sign of a man with a Type A personality (it is more difficult to pin down in a woman) is that he will urinate in the morning while cleaning his teeth – probably listening to the *Today* programme on Radio 4 into the bargain. There is no time to be lost in a Type A personality's life. His philosophy seems to be 'Dawdle, and someone else will rush past you towards the pot of gold.'

Recognizing the Type A personality
Before envying these Type A people with their ostentatious new cars, assured lifestyles and the apparent ease with which they have risen in their careers, take a good look at them. Satisfying their own and their parents' ambitions has inevitably brought untoward difficulties. They probably have gestures and tics that betray the stress that is boiling up within them. These tics and the problems they bring are dealt with in greater detail later in later chapters, but such gestures as clenching the jaw, tapping fingers and waggling feet are give-away clues to a life that is not as trouble-free as it may seem.

Type A people also need to dominate. Not only do they need to lead and rule at work, but they also need to control their home and social surroundings. Other people can't get a word in edgeways in a dinner-party conversation; if they are forced into silence from time to time as they eat the next mouthful and draw breath, they are never listening while others are talking, but are already planning their next *bon mot*. If silent while with a group of friends, they are probably preoccupied with their own thoughts – usually about how they can bring the conversation back to that which interests them and allows them to dominate and to shine.

The Type A personality can also be recognized in the supermarket. While this is not a favourite habitat for evolving executives or rising politicians, both successful and unsuccessful Type As have to use supermarkets occasionally. The Type A shopper rapidly calculates which queue at the checkout is moving fastest, and how much those ahead of them are carrying in each basket; trolleys are avoided. If their calculations are wrong, their impatience shows and they are mortified.

Similarly, Type A people in a motorway traffic jam are forever diving from one lane to another. When they have made it into whichever line of cars they hoped would be the fastest, they spend time checking the other vehicles to ensure that they haven't made a mistake – that someone else isn't doing better.

The key to understanding Type A people, as well as to helping them reduce the stress that plagues their lives, lies in understanding the motivation that drives them onwards and upwards into the chairman's seat – possibly with the occasional visit to the Priory Clinic thrown in. Type A personalities never seem to have enough time, and although they are doing several things concurrently, they are usually running behind schedule as they juggle their complex lives. Doctors who treat boardroom patients (or those who aspire to the boardroom) have a favourite question that assesses someone's stress level: they ask Type A people how many appointments they were late for or have had to cancel because they were overbooked and running behind schedule.

Unless stress is brought under control, the stressed Type A person is likely to become a patient, and furthermore, one who is prone to suffering from an overtaxed immune system, high blood pressure and heart disease, not to mention the likelihood of the metabolic disorder. The probability is that these problems will have been exacerbated by a life which has been so hurried or harried that they will have taken too little exercise, or exercise of the wrong sort. The ills determined by this level of activity (or lack of it) will have been compounded by a lifestyle that also ensures the sufferer is likely to eat and drink too much. As the waistband expands, so, too, do the chances of an early death.

Any Type A personality who wants to live to enjoy the material possessions and advantages brought by the hard-earned successes of early life must learn to control the stress that goes with it. These people must beat stress before it destroys them. They must learn to live with their personalities – just as anyone who has bought a wildly exuberant but potentially successful dog must learn to live with the dog's personality by training it so that it acts to its owner's advantage.

If people understand their own personalities, they will also understand the need to escape from them from time to time. They deserve and benefit from breaks when they can do things that provide relief from the treadmill to which they have sentenced themselves. Thus, every Type A with a hectic schedule needs to make opportunities to have a change of scene and pace. The long weekend is underrated as a therapeutic, stress-relieving respite. The secrets of the long weekend are to be away for at least three days and nights. If it is a two-night weekend, Saturday is spent worrying about what happened on Friday, and Sunday thinking of the best way to deal with Monday and the week ahead. Take Friday off, and the chain is broken.

What any relaxing weekend break for a Type A personality definitely should not include is an opportunity to sweat it out in the competitive atmosphere of a gym. In a modern gym, the corporate tyrants and obsessively ambitious have simply swapped their office desks for gymnasium equipment. Now, grim-faced and staring, they are either competing against others who are equally ambitious – or if their particular machine doesn't permit competition, they strive to beat their earlier performances. Each time they attend the gym, they will feel a failure unless they turn in a better performance than they did on the previous visit.

Are you a Type A?

Answer 'yes' to most of these questions, and it is highly likely that you are.

1 Are you always doing several jobs at once?

2 Are you obsessed with your work or your outside interests?

3 Are there never enough hours in the day to complete your overladen schedule or crammed diary?

4 Is your life planned with the exactitude of a Stalinist five-year plan? Are you goal-orientated?

5 Are you impatient?

6 Do you dominate the conversation?

7 Do you win the conversation – by bringing it round to a subject where you can shine?

8 Are you known for talking too quickly?

9 Do you eat quickly? Have you noticed that you
tend to finish your plate before your host or hostess?
Conversely, have you been so busy dominating
the conversation that you may be lagging behind?

10 Are you unhappy when you are relaxing?

11 Do you feel guilty about sitting around and
reading a book during the day?

12 Will you go to a cinema performance during
the day? (This is anathema to Type A personalities.)

13 Are you ruthless? Do you dispense with those
around you if they are interfering with your main
aims in life?

14 Do you select your long-term domestic partners
according to how they will help you in achieving
your aims?

Type B personalities

The opposite of a Type A personality is a Type B personality. This is neither a reflection on the Type B intellectual prowess nor certainly on their value to a family or community. They may not, on the other hand, be first choice to fill a vacancy in an American investment bank. There are highly intelligent Type Bs and rather stupid Type As. It is the approach to life that distinguishes the Type A from the Type B – not any inherent ability.

Nor do Type B people necessarily have the worst deal. They may well achieve a comfortable position that gives them a better and happier lifestyle than their Type A counterparts; for one thing, they are less likely to suffer stress.

The Type B he or she doesn't gallop through life, occasionally falling and sustaining some appalling injury, but instead, strolls through it and takes time off to contemplate. They have the time to stand and stare through windows. They also have the time to develop human relationships. They are not always thinking about any goals they are hoping to achieve – or haven't achieved. They may be lost in metaphysical thought. They are thinkers, even sometimes dreamers, rather than calculating doers.

It is said that whereas Type A people are full of anger, the Type Bs are easygoing and tolerant. Unlike the Type As, those people with a Type B personality experience a life that is not a never-ending struggle to achieve the maximum in the minimum time. Unlike the ambitious goal-orientated who are stimulated by the need to overcome difficulties and to conquer, the Type B is thoughtful, even-tempered, tolerant and contemplative.

You are likely to be a Type B personality if you answer 'yes' to the following questions.

1 Does it take a lot for you to lose your temper easily?

2 Are you as concerned with your family and friends as you are with your job?

3 Will you idle away the odd hour during the day, whether in the cinema or reading by the fire?

4 Do you react to situations, or do you plot to alter the situations so that they will suit your schemes? Type B people will make the best of what comes along, accept it, and sometimes do very well.

5 Are you creative or artistic, and do your friends regard you as a thinker?

6 Do you day-dream?

Type C and T personalities

As mentioned earlier, one change proposed by some psychologists that is helpful in understanding personality types and traits is to add two other categories to the classification: Type C and Type T personalities.

People with a Type C personality are born copers. They may not be the high-flyers in any particular job, but they are universally respected as a safe pair of hands and are considered to be utterly reliable. The world may be falling around their ears, their children may well be ill, their car may have broken down, the electricity has perhaps been cut off, and the stress may be such that everyone else would be so fraught that they would respond to the visit of a heavenly angel by biting its head off. Not so with the Type C personality. Despite all these problems, Type Cs can smile and cope, even if they are having to deal with 101 domestic problems. What is more, they may still be climbing slowly but surely up the career ladder.

In contrast, the Type T is a risk-taker – the 'T' in this case stands for 'thrills'. They are very different from Type C and Type B people but they may have much in common with the Type A personality, excluding any ability for successful forward planning. From a medical viewpoint, the 'T' in Type Ts also stand for 'testosterone'. Type T risk-takers are testosterone-rich, regardless of whether they are male or female.

Women as well as men have testosterone in their bodies; it is the balance between her testosterone and oestrogen levels that helps determine a woman's sense of adventure, her determination and her libido. It is said that the difference between a passive, timid woman and a risk-taking, dominant one is no more than the amount of testosterone equivalent to the glue on the back of a stamp.

Thus, Type Ts of either sex are thrill-seekers. If out riding, they can't see a high fence without wanting to jump it. They take up dangerous sports and undertake perilous journeys; they become ocean racers. These people are prepared to take risks with their own lives and the lives of other people. It is the risk that provides the thrill, and the thrill is all-important.

While Type C and Type T people are not so easily or clearly defined as those possessed of a Type A or Type B personality, Type T people do, however, display the symptoms of other well-recognized personality disorders. Many of these can be seen from an early age. Parents are usually very proud of their children if those who meet them in kindergarten, at children's tea parties or playing in the swimming pool report that their children are fearless. How often have I heard a parent say, 'I am told that my son or daughter doesn't know the meaning of fear.' The parent's face lights up with pride and pleasure. How unwise. These children may well have a lifetime of troubles ahead. A wise child psychiatrist once told me how his heart sank whenever he heard this expression. Over the years, he had found that no other symptom was a better predictor of a future stormy time for the little terror's family and friends.

Type T people are therefore stressed, but they laugh in the face of stress. The Type C personalities, who are so very different, are either born or influenced by events in early life to become compassionate, caring, coping people. They may be harried from morning to night and pillar to post, but they will take this stress and thrive. Of course, even the Type C will have a breaking point, but fortunately it will be rarely reached.

2
Physical symptoms
of stress

Stress and pain

No one is ever truly free of pain. At any one time, if people carefully think about their bodies, they will be aware that some part of their anatomy is aching. In some cases the aching is severe enough for it to warrant the description of 'hurting'. It is the constant shifting of aches and pains that prompts people to constantly fidget and shuffle about. This relieves their muscular discomfort and joint pains.

As a consequence of the constancy of minor bodily aches and pains, any anxious or depressed person is always able to find a symptom on which to focus his or her attention and project worries. Being over-concerned with the usual physical aches and pains that transitorily afflict humankind is therefore often a sign of anxiety. These symptoms may be induced by stress, or they may be evidence of some underlying depression. This phenomenon is especially a feature in those people who are hyper-conscientious or have Type A personalities. These are also the people who tend subconsciously to set themselves high standards. They can't bear to feel that all their troubles are the result of their personalities and so project their feelings of depression, anxiety and tension onto physical symptoms.

The Type A response

Physical symptoms are regarded as respectable by Type A people, but psychiatric symptoms, they misguidedly feel, are despicable. They dread the impact any talk of psychiatric disease or psychological problems might have on their work, for this has been the major influence on their lives. Work, the office and the life that spreads from it have been their emotional refuge. They don't want any suggestion that the stresses and strains it causes may be too much for them and that they would be better off pruning roses.

Ill-defined physical symptoms commonly associated with stress are also often a hidden manifestation of a depressive state. Fortunately, this type of depression in people with these personalities usually responds as if by magic to medication. Patients who have previously good, if obsessive and highly conscientious, personalities generally react well to drug therapy. As some of these symptoms may be related to excessive anxiety, and they can be part of the reaction to stress, cognitive therapy used in conjunction with medication may be useful.

A typical example of this phenomenon is that of chest pain, which is a frequent symptom in the GP's surgery and in the psychiatric clinic as well as in the chest physician's or cardiologist's out-patients examination room. A chest pain, which is in fact no more than the result of sitting slumped in an uncomfortable chair and is therefore of neuro-muscular origin, can and often is immediately misinterpreted by over-anxious people as the first sign of heart disease.

Likewise, a pain radiating down an arm that has stemmed from carrying a heavy briefcase (loaded with the details of the clients who keep the busy financier glued to his desk) isn't always or even usually a symptom of heart disease. It is more likely to stem from the pressure that has been put on the nerve plexus, or network, in the neck that supplies the arm. Even so, when interpreted by anxious or depressed people, such pain is, in their minds, another sure sign of incipient heart troubles.

Doctors are used to dealing with problems of this sort. There is rarely a day in a busy practice in which some patient will not be suffering symptoms of this kind. Although, if they are intelligent, patients will have made their own assessment of their condition, they will not be able to achieve the detached appreciation of the situation that is open to a doctor. The doctor has the advantage that his or her opinion will not be based on the experience of one patient, but on the great number of similar patients over the years who have consulted them and have had the same troubles.

Conversely, patients usually only have the experience of one case: their own. On this single history they will have to base their studies and make their opinions. People are worried that, when depressed, anxious, stressed and filled with feelings of worthlessness, they may be troubling the doctor unnecessarily. They fear that they are using up surgery time that should be available to those who they assume are more ill and worthier than they are. This idea is self-deprecating nonsense. Treating a depressive illness, or discussing the lifestyle that may have led to it as the result of the excessive stress this has engendered, is one of the most important roles that a doctor can fulfil. These people are also some of the most satisfying patients to treat, and watching them be restored to health within just a few weeks compensates for all those cases that haven't turned out so well.

Muscle pain

Experienced doctors can judge the mood of a patient the moment he or she enters the room. Sir William Osler, the father of modern British medicine, once said that a doctor who didn't already understand a patient's state of mind before he had completed the journey from the surgery door to the examination chair would starve. The doctor notices that the stressed or depressed patient has a very tense walk; the shoulders droop and are hunched forward. The stressed and depressed hold themselves differently and move differently from other people. They are not only hunched but their jaws are set tight. Patients who are very stressed clench their jaws so that the muscles over the angle of the jaw become very obvious. Really twitchy patients clench and relax the jaw, so that as you look at their faces, your eye is inevitably drawn to the angle of the jaw, where you can see the muscle moving under the skin. Anxious people's fists are held tight, and they don't sit still; instead, they swing their legs and tap and wiggle their feet. Patients who are disturbed are reluctant to look the doctor in the eye, but this is a symptom of many psychiatric conditions and not solely of depression or tension.

Holding muscles too taut uses energy unproductively. A day when someone who is tense may never have left his chair may still leave him tired. That is because the stressed patient is suffering from one of those conditions that renders them liable to be labelled 'tatti': medical parlance for 'tired all the time' syndrome, or TATT. The tatti patient is considered to epitomize the heartsick patient. Feeling tired the whole time may be the first symptom of some serious physical complaint, but it may also be only a reflection of persistent tension in the patient's muscles. This can keep the joints in a constant state of tension with no intervening periods of rest and rehabilitation.

Posture is maintained by the body's unconscious nervous system keeping the opposing muscle groups around the joint in equilibrium. In this way, a person can remain still and the minimum amount of energy will be expended. If the competing muscle groups are forever relaxing and tensing, the posture is only maintained if unnecessary amounts of energy are expended. The long-term effect of this fruitless battle between competing muscle groups around a joint is that the friction generated by this tension grinds the limbs together so that the cartilage cushions, which act as 'washers' within the joint, are constantly being eroded. This process produces pain and, in the long term, hastens the onset of osteoarthritis. In the short term, it causes the muscles to ache, puts a strain on ligaments and, if there is already any osteoarthritis in a joint, this tension exacerbates it and stimulates discomfort or even pain. It is little wonder that, after a day of mental stress, the muscles ache, the limbs are tired and the joints are painful.

If the great strap-like muscles that run alongside the spine and maintains its posture have been under tension, then the spinal joints can also be affected. The same tension will put the spinal joints and the disc spaces between them under pressure. A tensely held spine is likely to impinge on the nerves leading from the back and spinal cord. Any nerve route may have been, as patients often say, 'nipped'. A patient in whom there is nerve pressure will complain of a multitude of symptoms, including chest pain; exactly where the pain is felt will be dependent on the level of the disc giving rise to trouble by impinging on a nerve. At the largest medical screening line in the UK, the most common cause of chest pain was found to be that described as postural, neuro-muscular-induced pain, which may be caused by stress and tension coupled with an over-taut back.

If you answer 'yes' to the following questions, it may indicate that stress is producing symptoms which can lead ultimately to postural, neuro-muscular-induced pain.

1 Have you been holding yourself unnaturally tensely so that you feel that you simply must relax?

2 Do you ever feel that your jaw muscles are clenched?

3 Do you grind your teeth at night? Many patients who are tense not only clench their jaws by day, but also grind their teeth at night. I have known some patients who have ground their teeth so noisily that they have never married; they were ashamed of keeping their partner awake.

4 Do you ever find yourself drumming your fingers impatiently while listening to others?

5 Do you ever waggle your feet after crossing your legs? Do you tap the ground with your toes?

6 Do you ever screw your eyes up, no longer willing to listen to the opinions of others?

7 Do you have tension headaches?

8 If you do have headaches, do you feel that the pain stems from the over-tight muscles at the back of your neck? Does this pain extend from the neck to the area behind your eyes and to your forehead? These headaches are known as tension headaches, because they are so closely related to stress and anxiety.

Symptoms of anxiety

Those who suffer from excessive anxiety are not necessarily Type A people. Instead, they are very often highly strung, introspective, aesthetic people whose journey through life is a battle. In the nineteenth century, L. M. Willis, the wife of an American doctor, accurately described the usual passage of the anxious through life in the hymn 'Father hear the prayer we offer'. It is certain that those with excessive anxiety will never feel that they are forever in green pastures. As the hymn warns, they will have to persevere along steep and rugged pathways, and they will feel every stone along the way.

Unfortunately, it is those very patients who are genetically destined, or possibly have been conditioned by early life to be hypersensitive and easily upset by its changes and chances who have to follow a difficult road through life. They will find it almost impossible to tread rejoicingly.

If you answer 'yes' to the following questions, it may indicate that your personal stress has reached a level which results in physical symptoms.

1 Does your heart race without due cause?

2 Do you have palpitations? Are you conscious of your heartbeat?

3 When you put your head on the pillow do you hear your arteries beating?

4 Do you flush and blush more readily than usual?

5 Do you feel that you are sweating too readily?

6 Are you conscious of sweat trickling down your back?

7 Are your palms sweaty? Do you worry about having to shake hands with a stranger?

8 Do your feet sweat unusually? Do you make excuses so that you don't have to take your shoes and socks off in front of strangers?

9 Are you aware that you are sweating more under your arms than other people?

10 Conversely, are your hands and feet always cold, and is your nose as cold as that of the healthiest Labrador?

Heart problems versus anxiety

Since pre-biblical times, the effect of anxiety on circulation has been known and recorded. Some circulatory symptoms are more likely than others to worry a depressed, oversensitive patient. The following questions relate to circulatory problems that may result in symptoms which mistakenly, to the lay mind, could only be indicative of heart disease or stroke.

1 Have you been concerned about inexplicable chest pains?

2 Are you troubled by pains down your arms?

3 Do you have tingling in your arms?

4 Do you suffer headaches?

5 Do you have palpitations? Are you conscious of your heart beating?

6 Does your heart sometimes beat more quickly, and are you aware that its rate is increasing?

7 Do you ever seem to drop a beat from your heart?

If you answered 'yes' to some of these questions, don't be alarmed. Contrary to popular belief, most chest pain has nothing to do with the heart. The pain that comes from heart disease isn't a stabbing or shooting pain but a heavy, crushing, tight sensation. Some say it's as if someone is tightening a band – like a metal band around a barrel – around the chest. Others say that the chest pain stemming from a coronary thrombosis is similar to having a sack of concrete dumped on the chest. Anginal pain that is brought on by the temporary inadequacy of the oxygen supply to the heart muscles is of a cramp-like, constricting nature.

Unlike the anginal pain associated with a coronary thrombosis, exercise-induced angina soon passes once the patient has had a few moments' rest. Exercise-induced angina may also be triggered by emotion, whether of joy or anger. When heart pain that is normally induced by exercise or emotion in patients begins to be more easily induced, or if it starts to come on at rest, they should visit a doctor immediately. This may be a warning sign that serious trouble is in the offing.

The pain of a heart attack lasts longer than that of simple angina. The heart attack may have been precipitated by exercise or emotion; it usually comes on at rest, but it is not otherwise related. The heart-attack pain doesn't go as soon as the patient has rested, and it is associated with other symptoms. The person not only looks ill, but is shocked – sweaty, with a grey complexion – and feeling seriously ill. Even the pain from a heart attack doesn't, however, last for days or weeks like the pain of the over-conscientious, depressed, tense or worried person. Thus, when a patient says that pain has been present for a considerable length of time, it may have an important physical cause, but the good news is that it is unlikely to have originated in the heart muscles.

The effects of stress on breathing

Just as symptoms of cardiovascular dysfunction are often wrongly assumed to be the result of physical illness by stressed, tense or depressed people, other symptoms of stress result in breathing abnormalities. They may also be seized upon subconsciously as evidence of physical disease. In both instances, these symptoms may well provide evidence of someone with a depressed mood, as well as of someone who is suffering from unacceptably high levels of anxiety and tension.

In ninety-nine out of 100 cases, such symptoms as circumoral parasthesia (numbness around the mouth), tingling in your fingers and toes and even spasm in your hands and feet are *not* signs of an imminent stroke. To have a stroke is one of the persistent fears of anxious people, and it is one that may be heightened by the symptoms of hyperventilation. Fortunately, the tingling and spasm have nothing to do with strokes, but are caused by over-breathing, not disease. To correct the symptoms of subconscious panting (hyperventilation), breathe slowly and deeply for a time. An even more effective cure is to breathe in and out of a paper bag so that you re-inspire your expired breath. The symptoms then disappear like magic. NEVER USE A PLASTIC BAG.

Circum-oral numbness felt at a party is interesting. You may have attributed this to some unexpected side-effect of alcohol or to the amount you've drunk, but in fact, the principal cause is that, in the exuberant party atmosphere, you've been breathing more rapidly, talking more intensely and have actually been panting with excitement, although you might not have noticed it. Excess alcohol may play a part in inducing the sensation by increasing the respiratory rate, and even by having some neurological effect, but this is only a small factor. It's hyperventilation that causes it.

Carpo-pedal spasm – spasm in the hands and the feet – is a very weird and worrying feeling. It is never related to a stroke, but only occurs because hyperventilation has upset the natural biochemical balance of the body.

Typical symptoms of breathing troubles that may be brought on by tension are revealed by the following questions.

1 Have you noticed that you are breathing more rapidly, but despite this, you feel short of breath?

2 Do you ever take long, sighing respirations (air hunger) as you strive to relieve your hunger for air?

3 Do you feel out of breath, even though you have only been sitting in a chair and not exercising?

4 Have you noticed that when and if you have been hyperventilating, the skin around your lips feels fractionally numb? That you have circum-oral parasthesia?

5 Have you noticed that your fingers and toes tingle if you are breathing too rapidly as a result of your anxiety? (Parasthesia may not be confined to the lips.)

6 Even more alarming, have you been aware that, as well as the tingling in your hands and feet, you have also noticed that they are going into spasm?

7 Do you ever feel that everybody is talking from a great distance, rather as if you are swimming underwater in a pool, and friends are talking to you from the edge of that pool? This, too, can be a symptom of hyperventilation.

Sleep

A person's sleep pattern is all-important. A third of the day is spent asleep, a third at home and (to varying degrees) awake, and a third at work. The nature of someone's sleep is not only often the key to avoiding stress, but changes in the pattern of sleep frequently provide clues to discovering what has caused stress, if it is present.

People who don't sleep well are never at their best the next day; at best their work is not of the quality it might have been, and their enjoyment of the ordinary joys of life is reduced. At worst, sleeplessness at night can lead to inattention the next day, so that someone who is either driving a car or working machinery may suffer a sudden lapse of attention and have a disastrous accident. Not all insomnia has the same pattern, and the relationship between wakefulness and sleep, of the ease of going to sleep and the difficulty of getting up are all important pointers to someone's temperament and the pressures he or she may be suffering.

Doctors interviewing depressed patients are keen to uncover any evidence of the classic depressive state of mind. Sleep patterns are one of the important clues of this. Whereas anxious, worried patients can't get to sleep, depressed patients tend to drop off to sleep straight away as soon as their heads hit the pillow, only to wake up two or three hours later. Thereafter they lie awake until the dawn, before at last dropping off to sleep when it is time to get up. This is the true depressive pattern. Don't be put off by it. Depressed people are easiest to treat if they have the classic signs and symptoms of this type of depression. They respond well to the currently available anti-depressants.

Answering 'yes' to the following questions may indicate that your stress levels have begun to affect or are already affecting your sleep patterns.

1 Have you ever gone to bed, put your head on the pillow, and woken up with the alarm, seven and a half hours later?

2 Is the sound sleep of early childhood now just a memory? Can you remember when you had a night's sleep in which you didn't wake during the night?

3 Have you now developed an anxious person's sleep pattern? Depressed patients are not the only ones where the distinctive sleep rhythm is upset.

4 Are you tired when you go to bed, but once your head hits the pillow, you toss and turn while you think of the troubles of the day? If so, you may share the anxious person's aberrant sleep habits.

5 Have you ever had a *nuit blanche* – not a wink of sleep all night? This might be accepted without comment after some great trauma, but if it happens regularly, help is needed.

6 Once asleep, do you dream? Are your dreams usually happy ones? Can you remember ever having a happy, jolly dream, or are you more likely to be in some impossible position, with the train careering towards you so that you're unable to get out of the way, however hard you struggle? This is a typical dream of the stressed.

7 Even more commonly, a stressed or insecure person experiences a dream in which the train is due at the station, and one problem after another stops them from getting there on time. This dream denotes insecurity, anxiety and stress, whereas depressed, unhappy people tend to have frightening or over-vivid dreams.

8 Do you find it impossible to get up in the morning? Is dragging yourself from the security and comfort of the bed a daily battle? Of course, it may be that any excessive addiction to the comfort of the bed is because you are overtired rather than weary of life, but demanding too much sleep may also be a symptom of depression. Those who suffer this may be seeking to avoid the world and all its ills, which they blame for their depressed state.

Snoring

While it has little to do with the psyche, snoring may in fact be a sign of restlessness, and hence of inward tensions. Whatever its cause, snoring has a great deal to do with your physical health. It is too important to be no more than the basis of corny jokes. Snoring can produce severe social problems, both for the snorers and those around them, and be a significant medical sign.

For example, so far as longevity is concerned, snoring may be one of the early signs of future cardiovascular problems. 'Crescendo snoring' is when the snoring grows louder and louder until it ends in an an explosive snort. The breathing then stops for a moment, and all is quiet. This period during which breathing is briefly arrested is known as apnoea, and during it the sleeper wakes up momentarily. Because this cycle can occur many times a night, these regular, brief periods of wakefulness destroy the regular pattern of sleep, and the resulting broken rhythm of the crescendo snorer leaves him or her tired the whole of the following day.

Not only may this morning-after sleepiness take some of the pleasure out of professional and social life but it may also be enough to precipitate depression in vulnerable people. Certainly, it may make people so tired that it inevitably worsens the stresses from which they may already be suffering. This type of snoring is also an indication that the snorer's sleep pattern is so disturbed that his or her performance at various tasks next day is likely to be affected, and it is this aspect of crescendo snoring that makes it potentially dangerous for drivers.

Furthermore, for reasons not entirely understood, there is an increased incidence of heart disease, stroke and high blood pressure in crescendo snorers.

The following questions will help determine whether you or someone within earshot suffer from crescendo snoring.

1 When you or your partner snore, is the snoring regular and at an even pitch throughout the night, even if the decibels are excessive?

2 Does the snoring become progressively louder and louder until there is a pause in the snoring, and the person has a moment or two without breathing, before the cycle is repeated?

3 If you are inexplicably overtired during the day, do you know whether you were snoring at night? Apnoea is a common cause of unexplained tiredness that is often not diagnosed if people are sleeping by themselves, or if a partner is too polite to mention it.

Stress and the nervous system

Stress affects the smooth working of what is known as the autonomic (unconscious) nervous system. Everybody is aware of the nerves under their conscious command. These respond to impulses from the higher centres of the brain, and it is these impulses that control the person's limbs, speech and all other voluntary actions.

However, most bodily functions – and the organs which carry them out, hidden away in the chest, abdomen, pelvis or skull – are not consciously controlled. Their nerve supply comes from the autonomic nervous system, which continues to work and direct the organs that are essential for life without conscious intervention. The autonomic nervous system controls the heart, the blood vessels, and thus temperature-control and such actions as blushing, breathing, the digestive system and the guts, the filling (but not usually the emptying) of the bladder, and some but not all aspects of the reproductive system. It also controls such mundane and yet essential activities as sweating and salivation.

Although this aspect of the nervous system is not under our control, its action may be determined by our state of mind. The smooth running of the autonomic nervous system reflects the amount of stress someone is suffering, so any change that produces symptoms may be a measure of the tension in someone's life. When people are over-tense, the nervous system is disturbed. Symptoms of tension include sweating too readily, blushing too easily, and rushing to the lavatory too often. Some people may even find that, when especially anxious, their voices are rasping and their tongues are dry.

Most people will have noticed many (perhaps all) of these symptoms when they have been going through a difficult patch and are tense. The following questions allow you to check them for yourself.

1 Does your voice start to croak if your boss is especially threatening or trying, your colleagues are uncooperative, or your partner is seductive?

2 Do you sweat more readily than you would like to?

3 Does your heart race too readily?

4 Do you blush too often?

5 Can you sit throughout a cinema performance or a lunch or dinner without having to rush to the lavatory?

6 Do you feel the need to urinate even though you have just done so?

7 Do you suffer from the urgent need to urinate? This may at times be so acute, or the control of your bladder so disturbed by the effect of tension on autonomic bladder control, that when very anxious, or even very emotional, you might leak like an overexcited puppy.

Intestinal symptoms

In addition to the symptoms described on pages 40 and 41, an upset nervous system is also liable to affect the digestive and intestinal functions. For example, some stressed or anxious people have to go to the lavatory many times before they leave for work, but thereafter have normal bowel habits. Then there is the condition known as 'intestinal hurry': the result of an over-sensitized gastro-colic reflex. In lay language, this means that a heavy meal settling into the stomach – such as during a business lunch – stimulates activity throughout the length of the gastro-intestinal tract.

The more stressed and tense the person, or the more demanding the meal, the more sensitive the gastro-colic reflex becomes. This is why, when dining in a restaurant that specializes in upmarket business lunches where both business and social tensions collide, you will find few tables from which the younger and less assured don't disappear to relieve themselves before coffee. The combination of anxiety and eating is too much for their tense, stressed intestinal systems. So whether your guts are overactive or you are suffering undue sluggishness, the cause is an upset autonomic nervous system; its balance has gone.

Another obvious sign of stress is the loss of appetite, and the feeling of nausea after only a few mouthfuls. This particular symptom is especially obvious when the stress is brought on by romance. When people first dine with their newly acquired or potential lover, they often lose their appetites entirely.

If you answer 'yes' to the following questions, it may well indicate that stress is affecting your intestinal system.

1 Do you find that, when there are too many problems facing you and your peace of mind has been destroyed, your digestion is out of control?

2 Has your bowel activity ever seemed out of control first thing in the morning, but returned to normal for the rest of the day?

3 If having a business lunch, do you have to make a rush to the loo after, or even before, the coffee?

4 Conversely, have you suddenly become constipated, although your dietary habits remain unchanged?

Remember that a persistent change in bowel habit may be the first symptom of something more serious. If it lasts for more than two or three weeks, visit your doctor.

'It's not our job to prove you owe us £4,053.69;
it's _your_ job to prove you don't.'

3

Emotional and psychological symptoms of stress

Coping strategies and defence mechanisms

Even those who are not aware that they are stressed may have realized that all is not well with their lives and that their tendency to explode with anger and shout at the traffic warden is undesirable, not only because it will irritate all who hear it, but because it could be damaging them, the puce-faced shouters. Once they become aware of this, their body and mind will subconsciously, and perhaps with a bit of a push from their doctor, develop means of easing the stress. This subconscious method of handling stress is called a 'defence mechanism'.

On the conscious level, plans that are made to reduce stress are known as 'coping strategies'. Coping strategies are therefore the schemes, talked over at family dinners or when driving with a spouse or partner, to alter the pattern of life so that time is better planned and any subsequent irritations are soothed. Coping strategies can be divided into three groups:

1 'Damage limitation'. It is not always possible to exclude a particular source of stress, but it may be possible to reduce the emotional damage it causes. Means of managing the emotional consequences that the stress triggers have induced can be introduced.

2 Reduction. Other coping devices are designed to solve the problem so that the amount of stress is reduced. These are the lifestyle changes that all stress-reduction plans should include.

3 Change of approach. There may be less stress from a domestic or professionally unfavourable environment if the approach of the person to the stress can be changed.

'If it's my bank manager, tell him I'm in a new business meeting.'

Denial

Ordinary people with no special training outside their own disciplines may have to continue to function while their spouses may be shouting at them or their bank manager is constantly on the telephone, but once the formerly stressed person is able to deny or suppress the emotions that he or she really feels, everything may be well. An application of denial is to banish mental images or evidence of possible disasters that may be just around the corner. A classic example of this approach is that of the heavily debt-ridden person who refuses to open brown envelopes, preferring instead to leave them on the doormat. Such people know that they can't pay the bills, so what's the use of worrying about it? Instead, they simply hope that the bailiffs won't be sent in, but should this occur, they will handle the situation as it happens. Meanwhile, the person in denial will set about finding something more constructive than disorganized and destructive anxieties to occupy the time.

The role of repression

There is some evidence that men tend to devise carefully laid-out plans to deal with stress. Conversely, women, so it is said, are more likely to cope with stressful situations by ignoring them. This analysis assumes that women are more adept than men at repressing their feelings. Repression is the subconscious, involuntary dismissal of disturbing feelings and emotions, thereafter banishing them so that they may be hidden away in the unconscious. Unlike their female counterparts, men resort to coping strategies to help them to disregard or later forget disagreeable memories or thoughts when suppressing the fears engendered by seemingly overwhelming problems.

While the sexes would seem to differ in the forms their repression take, they all seem to deal with stress by denial, refusing to accept thoughts and feelings that they think are unacceptable. They are fantasists – just like a drunk who won't admit that he is drinking, or the unhappy worker who thinks that if only she could solve one particular problem, all would be well. In the case of those who are suppressing fears engendered by overwhelming problems, their denial and fantasy may even serve a useful purpose.

First revered, then reviled, Sigmund Freud is again being acknowledged as someone whose emphasis on the subconscious has left an important legacy to medicine. Very often the subconscious takes over when stress begins to become unbearable. Compensatory mechanisms, for instance, can actually be subconscious attempts to overcome any real or fancied inferiorities.

A sense of inferiority – an inner belief held by someone that he or she is intellectually, socially, racially, physically or sexually inferior – may be a great source of stress. Yet the very mechanisms that swing into action to relieve and compensate for any of these presumed inadequacies may in fact so subconsciously inspire and motivate some people that they may lie at the root of extreme ambition and often success. People who are compensating for a real or imagined deficit in one aspect of life may therefore strive to shine in another area without understanding the compulsion that drives them to do this.

Someone, for instance, who is not a natural athlete but would dearly love to have inherited athletic genes may find an outlet for his or her macho ambitions. They may never be able to play fly-half for their national rugby side; nature did not design them for this. They may also be too frail to succeed in any contact sport – but they *can* learn to sail. This experience will give them the necessary skills and muscular development. Given time, they may become supremely good sailors.

Fear of judgement

Much of the stress experienced in all branches of modern life, including the bedroom, is the result of the fear of judgement. When stuck for a question, many psychiatrists look at their patients and ask them earnestly, 'Who are you trying to please: your mother or your father?' This is primarily because everyone goes through life expecting to be judged, as they were judged by their parents; it is this fear of judgement that becomes the basis of the anxieties experienced by those who develop social phobias.

These are the people who dread going out; they are frightened that, if they do, then all eyes will turn to them, assessing them and all aspects of their lives. They will be judged, they feel, as to their poise, their clothes sense, their facial appearance, their sex appeal, their probable income and their hairstyle as they walk across a crowded hotel lounge, up the aisle of a church or stand to make a speech.

Guilt

The basis of the fear of judgement is that we all know ourselves very well, we are ashamed of what we know about ourselves, and live with the anxiety that something about our demeanour or appearance will betray our weaknesses. Even the toughest old roué has some feelings of guilt; he would simply rather not disclose the reasons for it.

It is fashionable when discussing stress to assess the amount of guilt people carry around in their baggage; thus, various tables have been devised to assess a person's guilt level. Answering 'yes' to the following questions should give you some idea of how much a burden of guilt you are currently carrying around on your shoulders.

1 Do you always assume that you are at fault – that whatever happens, you are to blame?

2 Once an incident – however embarrassing, however shaming, however badly you did – is over, are you able to forget it? Or does your mind return to it constantly?

3 Are you a hard judge of yourself? Are you tougher on yourself (and perhaps on your family) than on the rest of the world?

4 Do you forgive yourself or do you ruminate about what the prayer book describes as your 'multitude of sins and wickednesses'? Do you feel guilt about having done those things you shouldn't have done, as well as having left undone things you ought to have done?

5 Do you believe that you are responsible for other people's disasters? Was it your behaviour or your very existence that drove your parents to suicide, triggered their coronary thrombosis or brought on their stroke?

6 Do you look back and preface all your thoughts with the phrase 'If only I had...'?

7 Would you describe your sense of guilt (about fearing you might be responsible for the difficulties of others, and about your own failures) as being very damning, damning, minimal or non-existent?

8 Do you discuss your feelings of guilt, or are their origins so awful you don't mention them?

Assertiveness

Ten years or so ago, learning to be more assertive was rather fashionable. At that time, once polite and helpful colleagues disappeared for a weekend course subsidized by their employers and came back bloody-minded, stubborn and uncooperative. Unfortunately, only a fine line divides the quality of being assertive from that of being self-absorbed and rude. As a result, the need for people who are reasonably polite but also reasonably assertive has been played down. Assertiveness has become a joke, but lack of assertiveness is still a potent cause of stress.

At its most simplistic, being assertive is having the ability to say 'no' without fear that you will lose the regard of a friend, relative or colleague, but it goes beyond this. If you want to adopt an independent line, you have every right to do so – provided that you are not compromizing other people or hazarding the vulnerable. Lack of assertiveness is not just a female characteristic; it affects both sexes. Being too anxious to please others so that every decision is made only after considering the welfare of every other person and your own concerns have been ignored is a sure recipe for stress. Unfortunately, the stress from not being assertive is a fertile breeding ground for resentment. Martyrs probably went to the stake grumbling rather than singing.

Giving honest answers to the questions on the next page will give you an idea as to whether or not you are independent, assertive and fair, or are so assertive as to be bloody-minded and tiresome, if not an actual bully. They will also tell you whether you are so passive that you'll inevitably become stressed and resentful as every ghastly job is heaped onto your shoulders, your in-tray is never empty, yet despite all the extra work, no one takes any notice of your opinions.

1 Can you say 'no'? Can you refuse an invitation, task at work or in your home life without feeling guilty? Or do you feel honour-bound to produce a good reason for turning down any invitation or request other than that you have no desire to do it, or because it might upset existing plans?

2 Are you prepared to accept help from other people and ask for it? Lack of assertiveness is two-way. It is not just a question of never saying 'no'. It is also a matter of saying 'Please will you…?'.

3 If you've made an agreement, are you prepared to admit if it becomes impossible to fulfil? Would you ask for the contract to be re-negotiated? Are you prepared to admit making mistakes, including those concerning your ability to achieve an objective?

4 Are you indecisive, or conversely are you too timid to change your mind?

5 Do you fear success?

6 Are you so assertive that other people describe you as aggressive? Could you be passive-aggressive and dumb insolent? This is a fine art. Demands are stated, every pill is sugared but the pill the passive-aggressive person asks someone else to swallow is still bitter.

7 Do you ever use emotional blackmail? Do you bare your soul hoping that others will do things for you so as to avoid hurting you? Are you, in fact, manipulative?

The key to being assertive without being aggressive and uncooperative is to plan and carry out an appreciation of the task in hand. Know what needs to be achieved, choose one aspect of it that must be the primary objective and decide how it may be achieved. Having settled these basic boundaries, decide what is reasonable for you to do in order to achieve the objectives, and what is reasonable to ask others to do to help you in attaining your own goals.

The consequences of not formulating such a positively assertive plan of action are nowhere better seen than in the world of politics. Just as in other aspects of life, in politics, the aims of any group, and the roles of the people involved, are too often poorly defined. The rewards for working on the project – even the job description of those in the team – are frequently either casually thought through, or very often not thought through at all.

The 11 May strategy

Before NATO became all-important, army problems were solved by reference to a mnemonic device known as the 11 Mai, or 11 May. The breakdown of the letters is as follows.

The first '1', or 'I' stands for 'Intention': the primary intention, the goal. The second 'I' stands for 'Information': a careful explanation of the existing circumstances and how they have contributed to the need to achieve the primary intention. It is also necessary to explain how the achievement of that intention or goal will alter the situation for the letter.

'M' equals 'Method'. This is the explanation of the outline of the plan, and of everyone's role in it and how these different roles will contribute to the achievement of the primary intention. 'A' is about 'Administration'. Just who is going to provide what, where, when, why and how? Who is paying for it? Who is arranging the infrastructure? The final 'I' (or 'Y' as the Old English 'I' substitute) stands for 'Intercommunication'. How do you get in touch with everybody else involved in the plan?

You don't need to be in the army to benefit from this strategy. In any sort of team situation, by remember the 11 May mnemonic and using it as a format to present a strategy, the purpose of commands become plain; everyone is conscious of their role and should be satisfied that they have had a fair deal. If the team is reasonable, there will be no confusion, no aggression, no reliance on passivity with reluctant participants, and no coercion with manipulation; everybody will be happy and stress will be minimalized.

Another way of achieving the 11 May effect is to divide all problems into six steps and deal with each one in turn. This is a very clear-cut list, but since there is no way of remembering it, it has to be looked up before preparing an outline of any strategy.

1 Define the problem.

2 List the solutions.

3 Choose the best solution.

4 Plan to implement it.

5 Put the plans into operation.

6 Assess the result.

This mental drill has the disadvantage that, unlike the implication behind the use of 11 May, there is not the assumption that, if it is completed, success will follow automatically.

Four essential skills for stress-free planning

1 When discussing the method – the M of 11 May – define any delegation. Faulty delegation (either too much or too little) spreads stress faster than an outbreak of flu in an office. If you are in charge, it is your job to know how much you are going to do yourself and how much is going to be delegated while the goal is being achieved. Once delegated, how much supervision, if any, are you going to give to the people to whom tasks have been delegated? What is their responsibility; what's yours? One responsibility is inevitably yours: you must ensure that the programme is on time and is running smoothly.

2 Keep a diary. A good measure of stress is to go through a diary for the last few weeks, working out how often appointments have had to be moved, cancelled or cut short because the diary has become over-filled. Make certain your diary commitments are attainable. One of the greatest business tycoons of the century told me, and showed me the proof that confirmed this, that he never did more than four hours work in a day. Another successful company chief executive asked me to spend a day with him. I was astounded. He went into the office before anyone else and nosed around for an hour and a half. Later he met with all his departmental heads to get a feel of how their departments were performing, gave his opinions and orders and then left for the day. He reappeared in the late afternoon to see how well his commands had been carried out, and where adjustments would be needed. He and his secretary dealt with his

own correspondence, he saw anyone who had any problems, then he went home for an early gin and tonic. He was the first British vice-president of this particular international organization ever to become the overall chief executive in America. Diaries must always be left with enough spare space so that there is time to cope with the unexpected. Avoiding stress is often the ability to leave time for what Prime Minister Harold Macmillan called 'events, events, events'.

3 Take time off. Not just an hour or two, but give yourself a treat occasionally. Take a day away from the office. It doesn't matter what you do as long as it is to please yourself. Visit the theatre if this is what you enjoy. Find anything that is different from the normal routine, but make certain that nobody can trouble you and that you are answerable to no one – family, colleagues or friends.

4 Develop patience. One of the advantages of national service was that the army taught you to curb impatience and to wait without feeling irritation. The same lesson is essential for budding politicians, or for anyone who hopes to command. As a backbencher once said to me, parodying the title of an old film while we were waiting interminably for a minister and filling in the time with a gin and tonic or two, 'We also serve who only drink and wait.' Better than filling in time by drinking gin is to use it gainfully. Carry a book with you and take every opportunity to read it.

Stress and depression

As mentioned in chapter two, stress may trigger depression, anxiety or both of these. In all those who are depressed there is always an element of anxiety. Likewise, it is unusual for those who are anxious not to have some symptoms of depression. Even so, when considering patients' symptoms, an attempt should be made to separate the two groups of symptoms, as many of them are equally likely to be a feature of either condition. Some, however, will be more closely associated with one condition than the other.

If you are concerned about your stress levels, degree of anxiety, and your overriding moods, it is always worthwhile making an appointment to see your GP. Your GP is likely to ask you a string of questions; he or she will not only be interested in your answers but in *how* you answer. You can ask yourself the types of questions the doctor is likely to pose. Even if you have reached the state of mind where you either don't want to or even can't face up to the answers, try to be honest with yourself. If you don't question your own approach to life and ask yourself the necessary questions that expose your state of mind and improve your insight, it is less easy for anyone else to help you – and less easy for you to help yourself.

All of the following six questions are designed to reveal the hyper-conscientious, possibly obsessional person who is liable to set him- or herself very high standards and is liable to stressed or depressed if unable to achieve them. Answering 'yes' to them may well indicate that you are, in fact, a self-critical, over-conscientious worker.

1 Has your past medical history ever previously given any indication of psychological or psychiatric troubles?

2 Are you hyperconscientious, a perfectionist and worrier by nature?

3 Are you content with nothing but the best?

4 Do you strive to be a star performer, or are you content to be part of a team?

5 Are you a workaholic?

6 Do you always put your work first, even at the expense of your family and friends?

Other warning signs of excessive stress

1 Do you suspect that your family, friends and colleagues are talking critically about your behaviour?

2 Do those around you think you are relaxed?

3 Has your stress has reached the distressed stage?

4 Have you ever felt like crying for no apparent reason?

5 Do you dread the telephone, as it might be yet another person wanting something and you can't cope?

6 Do you complete the tasks you undertake?

7 Do you greet your children and family with the same affection and delight at seeing them as you did before? Can you still be bothered to play with your children?

8 If you have children, do you persuade them to disappear and leave you to your lonely thoughts?

9 Do you take as much trouble with your appearance as you used to?

10 If a man, do you shave daily and are your shoes clean?

11 If you are a woman, do you wear the same amount of makeup as you used to do?

12 Do you notice other people's clothes?

13 Do you still enjoy a night out?

14 How many previously enjoyable occasions have you cancelled recently because you can't be bothered to go?

15 Do you still take as much pleasure in your hobbies?

16 Do you look with the same delight at your most treasured possessions?

17 Does music enthuse you as much as it used to?

18 Do you feel guilty about enjoying yourself?

19 Do you think you haven't done as well as you should have with the cards that life has dealt you?

20 When you achieve something, do you immediately hope that it might impress or please others, over and above the satisfaction it might give you?

21 Are you able to refuse work, or are you too intent on either trying to please your boss or the bank manager?

22 Are you obsessed by planning your budget? Are you mean or profligate with your disposable income?

23 Have you found difficulties making up your mind? Does it take you longer than normal to choose a pair of shoes, which train to catch, what to choose from a menu?

24 Are your thoughts logical or going round in circles?

25 Are you nit-picking and hypercritical? Are you still a good judge of character? Do you still notice and are you pleased by the achievements of others?

26 Are you still interested in other people's careers?

If your answer to more than a few of these is 'yes', your life certainly needs to be re-planned. All these signs of stress and depression may be no more than an indication of the degree of tension that you are suffering; it may well be, however, that you are also depressed. In this event, the answers need careful analysis, as the degree of depression is important. This may be determined by which of the questions you say 'yes' to. If it is the underlying mood that is at fault, what you may need is not so much a lifestyle makeover but a visit to the doctor. He or she will be able to give you appropriate treatment, which may involve medication, often combined with cognitive therapy. Cognitive therapy is not deep psychotherapy; this is not always productive, whereas cognitive therapy doesn't delve too much into the past but helps you to realize your worth to other people, your strengths and attributes, and how you can re-plan your life to make use of them.

The emphasis in the first batch of questions is important because it has been found that people who have a highly conscientious personality with a medical history that has shown signs of psychological or psychiatric troubles still become depressed. If they do, the nature of their depressive symptoms is subtly different from those that affect other types of depression. Those who have an excessively conscientious personality, the type of person who hasn't had a day off work from eighteen to sixty-eight, are loath to admit that they might have psychological problems; these are for wimps, whereas real people only suffer physical problems. Their adherence to a strict work ethic (many are workaholics), and their highly tuned sense of duty makes them feel that any depressive feelings would be evidence of weakness. They're not going to have that. Instead, their subconscious readily comes into play and their symptoms are projected onto some relatively, if not entirely innocuous, physical symptom. This gives their minds an excuse to be ill.

The classic signs of depression

The human mind is always adept at protecting itself, subconsciously redirecting anxieties and fears away from the psyche and onto some physical symptom that unconsciously becomes exaggerated. One of my patients, for example, was a brilliant and hardworking successful City man. Arguably he was the leader of his particular City discipline; undeniably he had achieved eminence in the financial world. He wouldn't admit consciously to himself that his troubles were psychological rather than physical. What he didn't realize was that depression may well be cyclical. Each time he became depressed, he complained of symptoms that might well have occurred if he had some actual physical ill. When his depression lifted, all was well for a few years before he came back to see me with a new batch of symptoms.

It is important to recognize that the signs of depression are legion. They may often be an indication that stress from one aspect of life or another has become important – but this is rarely the whole story if a patient has the classic signs of an affective illness: one that affects mood. These people need treatment at the earliest opportunity.

Any one of the many symptoms of depression shown in the following questions is important, and each has to be evaluated on an individual basis. These symptoms may not only be precipitated by stress, but they may also be worsened by it. The symptoms are also analyzed so that the depth of a patient's depression may be assessed. Doctors especially take note of any suicidal thoughts, feelings of hopelessness, diurnal variation (that is to say, a lighter, more cheerful, positive mood in the morning than in the afternoon), loss of appetite, loss of weight, or any symptoms that might be indicative of psychotic change.

Symptoms of depression

1 Does life seem hopeless?

2 Do your problems seem insurmountable?

3 Do you blame your symptoms on other people?

4 Can you think your problems through carefully and logically, or do you rarely reach a conclusion?

5 Do your thoughts race around in a haphazard way? Are you, in fact, agitated?

6 Do you lack enthusiasm and zest for life?

7 Are you weepy? Do you find that you cry without an obvious reason?

8 Are your misery, lack of enthusiasm and feelings of hopelessness greater in the morning than they are later in the day?

9 If you have feelings of hopelessness, and a belief that nobody can do anything to help your situation, have you ever considered suicide?

10 If you have considered suicide, have you:
    a) Thought that life is not worth living: 'I might just as well be dead'?
    b) Considered if you would end your life?
    c) If you have considered killing yourself, have you decided how you would do it?
    d) If you have considered how you would commit suicide, have you made any specific preparations for it: hoarding pills, buying the rope, etc?

11 Has there been any change in your appetite?

12 If your appetite has changed, has it decreased? If so, have you lost at least half a stone in weight?

13 Has your appetite increased? If so, do you hanker after those so-called 'comfort foods': sweets, chocolate, puddings, or any foods with a high glycaemic index?

14 Do you drink alcohol more or less than usual? Alcohol intake may vary either way during depression.

15 Do you feel no longer concerned with other people's worries and emotions? Do you find it more difficult than usual to express love or gratitude to others? Have you or those around you noticed any emotional blunting?

16 Are you pleased to see people, or does their presence or telephone call merely irritate you?

17 Have you lost your sexual drive?

18 Are you smoking more?

19 How are you sleeping?

20 Do you:
  a) Go to sleep as soon as you put your head on the pillow, but wake again within an hour or two?
  b) Find it impossible to get off to sleep?
  c) If you have had a wakeful night, do you go to sleep just when it is time to get up?
  d) Do you sleep too much? Or find it impossible to get up in the morning?

'I've blown a fuse. I've never been to bed with anyone sexy before.'

4

Stress-related diseases

The stress response

All the many books written about stress include a chapter on what is known as 'the stress response'. Most people who have only patchy knowledge of neurotransmitters – substances which transmit the actions of nerves to cells – skim through it. Knowing about the stress response is important, but it is the *principle* of it that matters rather than the biochemical explanations.

The body has evolved over 150,000 years, and much of the time it has had to survive in unfriendly conditions. By the time it had grown sharp enough to avoid the sabre-tooth tiger or the woolly mammoth, we had already developed a sophisticated defence mechanism. Once alarmed, the body needed to issue an emergency directive. Survival depended on one of two responses: either its best purposes would be served by running away, which meant it needed to make use of its 'flight response', the mechanism that allowed it to flee from the sharp teeth or trampling feet of the wild animals living around it; or the danger might come from some other primitive people, in which case our ancestors would have needed to stand their ground and fight.

The stress response today

The fact that we are here today, reading this book, shows that our particular ancestors had a well-developed flight or fight response and survived generation after generation. The result is that we now survive to live in the cosseted world of the twenty-first century. Even so, we have kept our flight and fight responses, although they were tuned to respond to the sudden appearance of a wild animal in a primeval woodland. Instead, they are now needed to help us escape the traffic hurtling down the road, or to withstand the savage onslaught of the aggrieved boss or the furious jealousy of a scorned partner. Fear, anger and rage all excite the stress response. Sometimes the body, when alarmed, will immediately prepare for fight, and other times flight will be better.

Whatever we might think of the stressful conditions of modern life – the life-threatening circumstances, the aggression that may upset or hazard our lives – the hormones and neurotransmitters released into the system are of a strength that was designed to cope with the sudden danger of a sabre-toothed tiger and the woolly mammoth, not the persistent bully in the accounts department or a jealous, predatory colleague.

How stress controls the nervous system
As mentioned in the previous chapter (see page 40), the autonomic nervous system – that part of the nervous system that works without conscious intervention – controls the body's essential organs: the heart, the blood vessels, and the other bodily functions including the intestines, the bladder, the lungs (these are also partially under voluntary control), the sweat glands and flushing. Whenever humans are stressed, it is these organs and bodily systems that are alerted and prepared for the flight or fight response.

Modern life is unnatural. There is not a quick dash for cover and then either all is well or ancient man has become the tiger's breakfast. Modern man's stresses are constant: day after day, year after year. Husbands or wives are tricky, even difficult;

colleagues are impossible; bank managers are lacking in understanding. The stress of the twenty-first century is never-ending, and this means that the autonomic nervous system is never off-duty. In a life that is perpetually stressed, message after message reaches it, preparing it for the latter-day equivalents of flight or fight. This causes problems, because the body is not adapted to receive this ever-flowing series of commands.

As a result of withstanding a persistent barrage designed to prepare it for physical activity, the human body instead has to continue sitting in a chair, smiling blandly with no means of working off the chemicals that are now flowing around it. The only release for those who are subjected to such tensions is an occasional outburst of anger when the boss has left the room or wild, erratic, dangerous driving along the motorway. A continually alerted primitive survival mechanism that results in a highly sophisticated, static response has given rise to the twenty-first-century epidemic of stress-related diseases, some physical, some psychological.

Cardiovascular stress diseases

The primitive stress response, instigated by the action of the sympathetic part of the autonomic nervous system, prepares the heart and the blood vessels for action. It accelerates heart rate, constricts the blood supply to inessential parts and increases it to the heart muscles and limbs while the spleen contracts to top up the blood supply from its reserves. The autonomic nervous system also dries the mouth, stills the guts, increases sweating and mobilizes sugars and fats so that there is plenty of energy available to fight or flee. To some extent, the parasympathetic effect of the autonomic nervous system acts in a contrary way. It conserves energy, aids digestion and takes some of the load off the heart.

Just as the cardiovascular system was the target for the flight or fight response in primitive man, it is the target for today's stresses and strains. Some of the first physical signs of the over-stressed person are apparent in the arteries. Patients are too easily pleased with the state of their arteries; provided that the blood is flowing through them, they rest assured that their absurd lifestyle has not damaged them. However, modern science, in the form of an External Beam CT scan (EBCT), can measure the amount of calcium and fat-laden deposits, or atheromas, collecting in the wall of the artery, which in time will ooze into the arterial lumen (channel).

At first, these lumps will adhere to the inside of the arterial wall; later they may either grow across the artery and progressively obstruct it – thereby denying oxygen and other nutrients to the heart muscle, and causing angina once the patient exercises. Conversely, the lump may rupture and its fatty contents may escape into the circulation in clots known as thrombi. If a thrombus blocks one of the coronary arteries, the patient suffers what is known as a coronary thrombosis or myocardial infarction: the destruction of an area of heart muscle once its blood supply is obstructed. A myocardial infarction, or MI, is the sudden heart attack that all too often is fatal.

High blood pressure

Even as the arteries are narrowing or becoming clogged by atheroma which has formed as a result of the metabolic disturbances set in motion by stress, a life that is constantly full of tension causes hardening and constriction of those same arteries, resulting in a rise in the blood pressure. High blood pressure – known, appropriately, as hypertension – may lead to strokes, heart attacks and sometimes kidney failure or even retinal damage to the eyes. High blood pressure is another consequence of the stressed life.

Strokes

A stroke is any condition which, by interfering with the blood supply to the different parts of the brain, causes paralysis or some evidence of upset of the brain's normal function. There are two main types of stroke. The most common form is known as the ischaemic stroke. In the ischaemic stroke, the lumen of the cerebral blood vessel is blocked by a thrombus so that a cerebral infarction (death of part of that part of the brain supplied by the artery) follows.

A transitory stroke, which is one in which the symptoms last less than a day, is known as a transient ischaemic attack, or TIA. In this case, the blood vessel wasn't blocked by a thrombus that became lodged, but by a clot that passed on. Under a quarter of strokes are not caused by thrombi blocking an artery but by a haemorrhage (bleed) from a cerebral vessel that has ruptured; thus high blood pressure followed by a stroke is a frequent sequel to a lifetime of stress.

Aortic aneurysm

One cardiovascular disease that is too often overlooked is the aortic aneurysm, which is frequently the result of stress, high blood pressure and, above all, smoking. The aorta is the main blood vessel that leads from the heart – like the principal motorway leading from a capital city. If the blood pressure is raised, the walls of the aorta are subjected to increased pressure, and in all probability they will have already been weakened by atherosclerosis.

Rupture of the aorta is one of the most alarming of emergencies. Patients are always fortunate to survive. People who have had high blood pressure for a long time, or have a family history of aortic aneurysms, especially if they have ever smoked, should have their aortas checked by ultrasound examination at regular intervals. If the first signs of the dilatation of the aorta can be detected early once the aneurysm is large enough, the damaged patch – which may look rather like the weak patch on a bicycle inner tube – can be replaced by an artificial graft.

Metabolic effects of stress

As the autonomic nervous system prepares the tense person for the battles or retreats of modern living, it also alters the metabolism so that the muscles are supplied with energy. Crucial to metabolism in all cells is insulin, which allows sugar to be metabolized, thereby providing necessary energy. This is exactly why the tense, anxious person is often sweet-toothed or alchohol-loving. Alchohol, even without the mixer, is rich in sugars, and they have a high glycaemic index – that is to say, the sugar is readily absorbed into the circulation.

The result of the blood sugar rising rapidly after a couple of gin and tonics and a Mars bar is that the pancreas needs to produce additional insulin so that the blood sugar level may return closer to its normal level. Unfortunately, the pancreas always overreacts, producing a surfeit of insulin, and the blood sugar subsequently falls below its pre-snack level. Every cell in the human body is influenced by insulin. If this cycle is repeated, the body's cells are so frequently bombarded by insulin that they begin to develop insulin resistence. This can lead to the condition known as the metabolic syndrome.

The pancreas, the body's insulin factory, can only produce so much insulin. Initially production goes up to meet demand, but the amount of insulin is not limitless. In time, the combination of insulin-resistance in the tissues and an overworked and failing pancreas results in real or relative insulin deficiency and the development of what is called Type II (or sometimes maturity-onset) diabetes.

Diabetes

To what extent Type II diabetes is a direct consequence of stress and what extent it is the indirect consequence of a stressed person's over-indulgence in comfort eating is uncertain. But, whatever the mechanics of the process, stressed people often put on weight and often develop Type II diabetes as a result of their tense lives.

In time, the metabolic syndrome develops, and with it, Type II diabetes that leads to dangerously high levels of cholesterol, including the pernicious low-density-lipoprotein (otherwise known as LDL) cholesterol, kidney disease, neuropathy (nerve damage), diseases of the eye, including retinopathy and increased incidence of cataracts. In women, the metabolic syndrome may result in obesity, hirsutism (bodily hairiness), male pattern baldness, acne and ovarian cysts. These women also have other gynaecological problems, such as scant periods, irregular ovulation and infertility. There is also, in both sexes, an increased risk of heart and vascular diseases.

Although there is a strong genetic factor determining the likely development of the metabolic syndrome, much can be done to make certain that this genetic tendency isn't expressed. People are less likely to develop it – whoever their parents are – if they keep their weight down. Therefore a woman's waist measurement should be under thirty-two inches, and a man's under forty inches. The other crucial preventative factor is regular exercise.

Muscular effects of stress

As has been noted in chapter 2 (see pages 22–27), the stressed and depressed hold themselves quite differently and also move differently from other people due to the constant tension that is affecting their muscles. This build-up of tension can cause all sorts of pain in the body of the stressed.

Headaches and tension

The tension caused by generalized anxiety results in headache, both tension headaches and migraine; anything that may increase tension is likely to precipitate migraine. Migraine is the type of headache that follows a contraction of the blood vessels in the brain, followed by over-dilatation of them. At the stage of constriction of the blood vessels, there are often 'fortification spectra' – lines, dots, dashes, wavy vision. Other people may notice a transitory weakness in a limb.

Once the blood vessels have dilated, the brain becomes swollen and there is a throbbing headache, nausea and sometimes actual vomiting. The acute attacks may be cut short by taking drugs that alter this pattern of blood-vessel constriction followed by dilatation. They cause a long-lasting constriction so that the other symptoms never follow; for this reason, they are not prescribed for people who suffer from narrowed coronary arteries.

There are few compensations for growing older, but one of them is that the nature of migraines experienced by a sufferer changes. A patient whose brain has begun to shrink suffers the preliminary symptoms, but since there is room for the shrunken brain to expand within the skull, they avoid the throbbing headache and the nausea (similarly, hangovers are no longer accompanied by a splitting headache the next day).

Tension headaches are a different problem. They stem from holding the muscles in the back of the neck too tight. If there is any wear and tear in the joints in the neck, this compounds the muscular ache. See pages 25–26.

Back pain
Just as tension and stress put a strain on the joints in the neck, so they do in those of the back. Any disc lesion, such as a prolapsed intervertebral disc, will give rise to trouble if the back is held too stiff and awkwardly. Many patients with backache swear by exercises to help their problems. One of the causes why these may be useful is the relaxation that follows the exercises. See pages 204–215.

Gastro-intestinal disorders

For generations, stress was blamed for duodenal and gastric ulcers. It is now known that the principle cause of these diseases is infection with an organism known as *Helicobacter pylori*, and not the result of suffering in silence for years from the burdens of a pressurized and put-upon life. While this discovery has been a revolutionary step forward in treatment of the troubles of the gut, it has had one disadvantage. It has tended to obscure the importance of stress as a cause of other gastro-intestinal problems.

Nausea and vomiting may be associated with gastritis, and may well be an early symptom of anxiety and tension. The guts may also be overactive or underactive during periods of tension. If the sympathetic effects of the autonomic nervous system predominate, as described in chapter 2 (see pages 42–43), then there is a decreased movement of the guts. If the para-sympathetic effects are in the ascendancy, there are increased gut movements.

The anxious patient usually complains of diarrhoea and 'intestinal hurry'; the increased movement of the gastro-intestinal tract results in a sensitive gastro-colic reflex. No sooner does someone complete a meal than the distension of the stomach causes reflex movements throughout the guts and creates the need to visit the lavatory. This is the origin of the old soldiers' term 'windy', meaning frightened or over-anxious. If too afraid, a soldier's guts were unreliable, and excessive wind (or worse) might be the consequence. By 1939, society had become less euphemistic, and the description 's**t-scared' had largely replaced it.

Pre-menstrual tension

There is an association between pre-menstrual syndrome and stress and anxiety. As in many aspects of medicine, there is inevitably debate about which comes first. Do tense people develop PMS, or do those with PMS become tense? The latter event is certainly true. Whether there is any distinctive type of personality that suffers from PMS is uncertain. Only five percent of women are completely free from pre-menstrual symptoms, which makes it difficult to draw hard and fast conclusions.

In primary PMS, patients suffer physical, psychological and distinctive behavioural symptoms that tend to recur with each cycle. The greater danger to correct diagnosis of PMS is that a psychological or psychiatric condition from which a woman is suffering may be misdiagnosed as PMS, and thus she may be denied the treatment that would have corrected this. The only treatment that is of proven benefit are the SSRI or 5HT re-uptake inhibitors: the antidepressants. These work by increasing the amount of various naturally occurring chemicals by delaying (inhibiting) the reabsorption. The most often prescribed is Prozac. Other patients swear by Femal, made from the pollen of a particular form of rye grass; vitamin B_6; or oil of evening primrose.

'She's being a bitch. I put it down to PMT.'

Emotional, psychological and psychiatric disorders

Stress and anxiety states are closely interlinked, which is why, when many people discuss psychological disorders or psychiatric disease, the diagnosis is frequently veiled in the euphemistic term 'nervous breakdown'. Nervous breakdown isn't a medical description but a term that is used by the general public to cover many different eventualities. When someone's psyche does crack under pressure – the amount of pressure will depend upon the person's previous personality and his or her genetic make-up – the crack doesn't take some particular form by chance. The crack will occur down pre-determined lines – just as earthquakes will not strike in every part of the world, but only in those countries where there are geological features that give rise to fault lines.

Nervous breakdowns cause symptoms that could be predicted if someone knew the patient well. A nervous breakdown may therefore be a socially acceptable term to describe the condition of someone who has had an acute psychotic breakdown, a relapse of schizophrenia, or an attack of an affective disorder such as depression or mania.

Suicide can be a feature of any serious mental condition, but it is especially liable to affect those who have a psychotic disease or severe depression. In the cases of those who have simply needed time off because their anxieties finally weighed them down, anxiety states in the absence of depression or a psychosis are less likely to pose a suicide risk – but even so, such a risk still exists.

Eating disorders

Among the emotional and psychological conditions that are associated with stress, often of a very subtle sort, are eating disorders. Not only obesity, but problems such as also anorexia nervosa and bulimia often have a psychological base. The exact relationship between personality type and these diseases is contentious, but undoubtedly stress is a factor in them.

GAD

Unlike the blanket term nervous breakdown, which has no true medical meaning, a condition known as generalized anxiety disorder (GAD) is now recognized as a separate complaint. It results from the over-activity of the nervous system that causes the well-known syndrome of symptoms such as palpitations, hot flushes, sweating, trembling and dry mouth. The chest symptoms are the same as those brought on by stress, and include breathlessness, tingling in the limbs, difficulty in swallowing, nausea and intestinal upsets.

The person's mental state is also affected so that they feel dizzy; there is de-realization and de-personalization, i.e. it seems either that objects are unreal or that the person is separated from his or her own body, is looking down on it from a height and isn't really here. GAD suffers may faint. And just as in any real severe anxiety disorder, where there is an element of the panic response, there is also a fear of death.

Panic attacks

One aspect of stress is the increased liability to panic attacks and other panic disorders. Panic attacks are short-lived episodes of acute anxiety. Even if they only last for a comparatively short time, they are enough to leave the patient feeling mentally and physically exhausted. Psychiatrists won't diagnose a panic disorder unless a patient already has four of the common signs or symptoms associated with GAD – the symptoms listed under those that are the hallmarks of both long-standing stress and GAD.

The Greeks were not constrained in this way, as shown by the etymology of our modern word 'panic'. Pan was the Greek god of pastures, forest, fertility, flocks and herds. Half-man and half-goat, he had an overdeveloped libido and was accustomed to hide in remote spots in the mountains where he would suddenly pounce out upon the unwary traveller. Not unnaturally, these travellers suffered 'acute episodes of intense anxiety'. They didn't need to have had any previous history of troubles to be diagnosed as being in a state of 'panic' – a state of mind derived from the actions of the god Pan.

Only five percent of the population suffers from GAD, and with it, a tendency to panic disorders, yet a third of people at some time or another during their lives have had a panic attack. Ten percent have had more than one episode. Often it is a panic attack that initially drives a patient with a long-standing anxiety disorder to the doctor's surgery to discuss the situation. A characteristic of a panic attack is that it is usually impossible for the patient to do much about the precipitating cause. Doctors always bear in mind that anxiety disorders and panic disorders are not only closely related to each other, but they are also related to depression. Sixty percent of patients who suffer panic attacks are also depressed from time to time.

Phobias

A phobia is an especially strong fear that is triggered by some specific event or thing. There are a great number of phobias, but most people are aware of agoraphobia (a fear of open spaces or crowds) and claustrophobia (a fear of confined spaces). In both instances the patient is unable to see a ready route for escape. Other people fear other situations, such as the dark or flying. Apart from the situational phobias there are also those known as the 'animal phobias', including such conditions as arachnophobia – a fear of spiders – while others may have an unreasonable fear of dogs or of birds. Social phobias include a dread of meeting people or having to perform in public. The list is endless.

One particular phobia – the fear of flying – deserves special mention as it can be a limiting factor to peoples' lives. It restricts family holidays, and it makes it difficult to visit siblings or friends who have moved overseas. Terrorism has perhaps produced a reasonable aspect to the fear of flying, but even before terrorism, the dread, fear and acute anxiety state flying induced was quite out of proportion to the risk involved.

Cures for the fear of flying range from lavender armbands to a double whisky before take-off. A more rational approach is to have psychotherapy. There are courses run to treat a fear of flying in which the members of the group become acclimatized to the idea until it is finally acceptable to them; then they all fly off to celebrate their recovery.

The standard method of treating phobias is either to desensitize phobic people by gradually exposing them more and more to their feared object or happening, or to use 'flooding'. The latter is the psychiatric equivalent of throwing people in at the deep end. They are confronted by their fears, overcome them (it is assumed) and, it is hoped, thereafter are never so bad again. I've always favoured gradual desensitization.

*'Exercise is a great stress-buster,
Miss Agnew.'*

5

How stressed are you?

When people are aware of being stressed, they should make efforts to manage it. If motivated by the thought of reducing the dangerous effects of stress on the heart and cardiovascular system, the amount of will-power and insight needed will depend on their age.

When young, death seems a long way off. Even the obese twenty-year-olds who work twenty hours a day, drink more than the approved daily ration, smoke, never commit to a lasting relationship, and take no exercise will assume that the price is unlikely to be paid for twenty years. If they have a Type A personality, even plans to reduce stress won't satisfy their competitive instincts.

Older people, on the other hand, can already see Charon's ferryboat waiting for them to cross the Styx. It doesn't require so much to persuade older people to alter their lifestyles in order to reduce stress. In any case, by the time some agree to this, they may already have developed evidence of stress-related diseases.

Until recently, doctors were equipped only with comparatively primitive diagnostic tools to detect the first signs and symptoms of stress-related disease. It was difficult to persuade patients that apparently nannying old doctors knew what they were talking about, and that their advice had validity. Thankfully, this attitude is changing. It is now much more impressive to say to a patient, 'These include the EBCT (Electron Beam CT) scans of your cardiovascular system. They show that you have accumulated the atherosclerosis of someone twenty years older than you are.' (Atherosclerosis is the fatty substance that furs up arteries.)

From the mid-thirties onwards, unreformed Type A people could plot the early signs of the long-term stress that will get them in the end. With EBCT scanning, younger people, as well as those of more advanced years, will be able to heed these warnings.

Psychological stress-testing

A well-established and much-quoted psychological scale assesses the stress brought about by various major life changes. It was devised by Dr Thomas Holmes and Dr Richard Rahe in 1967. Admittedly, their values reflect the values of the United States and of an earlier generation; suitably modified, however, the concepts are still true. In Holmes and Rahe's index, the stressful, life-changing disasters that may beset anyone vary from milestones such as the divorce or death of a partner to the commonplace and trivial, such as the approach of Christmas, holidays or trouble for children at school.

It is probable that divorce is no longer quite as devastating as it was over forty years ago; losing a job, stressful as it is, is now a more frequent occurrence, and only becomes highly stressful if it is associated either with someone's age, so that further employment is unlikely, or as part of a general unemployment pattern in a neighbourhood, so that finding another job will pose serious problems. In these days of debt and mortgage, financial troubles may well figure higher in the list. In the original rating, taking out a mortgage, trouble with a mortgage company or difficulties with a bank were ranked as only slightly more important than change in responsibilities at work. Imprisonment is probably now more stressful than it was, as mob rule in prison replaces iron discipline.

Since the Holmes and Rahe index first appeared, people have been evaluating their points. I have reproduced the scale on the following pages so that you can evaluate your own rating based on their criteria. Score more than 100 points in any twelve-month period, and these psychologists maintain that you have a markedly increased risk of suffering from a major illness in the next two years.

The Holmes and Rahe Social Readjustment Rating Scale

Life Event

Death of spouse	100
Divorce	73
Marital separation	65
Imprisonment	63
Death of close family member	63
Personal injury or illness	53
Marriage	50
Dismissal from work	47
Marital reconciliation	45
Retirement	45
Change in health of family member	44
Pregnancy	40
Sex difficulties	39
Gain of new family member	39
Business readjustment	39
Change in financial state	38
Change in number of arguments with spouse	35
Major mortgage	32
Foreclosure of mortgage or loan	30
Change in responsibilities at work	29

Son or daughter leaving home	29
Trouble with in-laws	29
Outstanding personal achievement	28
Wife begins or stops work	26
Begin or end school	26
Change in living conditions	25
Revision of personal habits	24
Trouble with boss	23
Change in work hours or conditions	20
Change in residence	20
Change in schools	20
Change in recreation	19
Change in church activities	19
Minor mortgage or loan	17
Change in sleeping habits	16
Change in number of family reunions	15
Change in eating habits	15
Vacation	13
Christmas	12
Minor violations of the law	11

Readers should also read the following questions which are roughly based on work by Dr Audrey Livingston Booth (see bibliography, page 220). They have been modified to fit into the twenty-first-century. Readers should reply to each question either 'often', 'not often' or 'rarely'. A well-orientated individual who is not being driven off-course by too stressful a life, should answer 'often' to every question.

To detect the state of your emotional health and the extent that stress is affecting it, answer these few straightforward questions. How many times recently have you:

1 Really laughed out loud (truly genuine laughter and not a BBC-audience feigned guffaw)?

2 Shown really deep, caring affection for your friends?

3 Felt deeply emotional about music – or whatever moves you?

4 Enjoyed a satisfying sexual relationship with someone?

To assess the state of your social life, answer the following. How many times lately have you:

1 Entertained friends other than business associates in your own house?

2 Been in contact with friends who live far away?

3 Contacted your brothers, sisters and parents?

4 Contacted more distant relatives?

To assess the state of your intellectual equanimity, answer the following. How many times lately have you:

1 Felt really stimulated intellectually in your job?

2 Enjoyed the stimulus of a serious discussion with friends even if you may not be in agreement?

3 Become involved in interests outside your work?

To assess the state of your physical health, answer the following. How many times lately have you:

1 Sat down at the family table and enjoyed a good breakfast?

2 Have taken half an hour off for relaxation before lunch? (It is hard to remember that, even within my lifetime, this used to be standard practice.)

3 Walked briskly up the stairs instead of taking the lift?

4 Walked a brisk two miles or at least forty minutes?

5 Been swimming?

6 Walked for five or ten minutes before bedtime? (Although this is good for the levels of your blood fats, it is not recommended for the insomniacs of the world.)

The stressed body

Hair
Extreme stress, or disease, may cause hair to be shed. Clumps of hair may then be found on bed-pillows. New hair doesn't grow to replace old hair, which is always dying off.

Brain
When the brain senses a threat, it activates the flight or fight response, producing hormones, including steroids such as cortisol. In time, the body's ability to produce cortisol at this rate fails and stress symptoms begin to appear.

Mouth and throat
Symptoms include frequent sore throats and mouth ulcers. Stress undermines the body's immune system so it becomes more prone to infections.

Neck
Tension headaches stem from a neck that is held too rigidly. Nerves are subject to pressure, the muscles are held rigid, and the result is the painful classic tension headache.

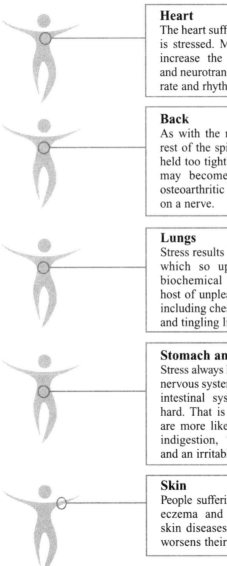

Heart
The heart suffers when a person is stressed. Metabolic changes increase the blood-fat levels, and neurotransmitters affect the rate and rhythm of the heart.

Back
As with the neck, so with the rest of the spine. If the back is held too tightly, any worn joint may become painful, or its osteoarthritic spikes may press on a nerve.

Lungs
Stress results in over-breathing, which so upsets the body's biochemical balance that a host of unpleasant side-effects, including chest pain, air hunger and tingling limbs, occur.

Stomach and guts
Stress always hits the autonomic nervous system (and with it, the intestinal system) particularly hard. That is why the stressed are more likely to suffer from indigestion, 'intestinal hurry' and an irritable bowel.

Skin
People suffering from psoriasis, eczema and a host of other skin diseases know that stress worsens their condition.

'You may as well relax, Henry. I know what you want and you're not getting it.'

6

Life's stressful
events and situations

Bereavement

Bereavement may be induced by anything that creates a severe sense of loss. The death of a close relative or beloved friend and divorce are both triggers for the bereavement response. A person whose treasured house or art collection has been burnt may suffer as much bereavement as they would have done had a loved relative died. While a person is dying, the grieving for those who will be left behind is already beginning. Family and friends are beginning to re-adapt their lives so as to be able to live without the person, but they are already suffering the pangs of separation. This is one of the problems of sudden death. Sudden death not only reminds everyone of their own mortality but also removes the pre-death grieving. How many times have I heard something along the lines of, 'I was standing there talking to her, doctor; she seemed perfectly all right and we were planning what to do next weekend, when suddenly she said she felt rather tired and collapsed in front of me'?

Sudden death is therefore especially distressing because there is no way in which a family can become accustomed to it. The grief response is a phased one. Even when the death is expected, the reality that someone will have to do without a spouse or a child is more than their psyche can bear; thus, the first stage is often one of denial. In both world wars, many parents were like Rudyard Kipling, often taking years to accept that their sons had been killed and continuing to expect them to return. Others, like Queen Victoria, continue to keep the house and regime just as if their beloved is still alive. It is common for those who have recently been bereaved to have delusions and usually to hear or occasionally to think they have seen the dead person around the house.

'Funerals are much less stressful than weddings.
Everyone cries at weddings.'

The next phase in the grief process is anger and blame. No sooner is a tragedy reported in the papers than there is news that the bereaved are blaming and suing someone for what was often an unfortunate but understandable accident or merely a nasty trick of nature. Doctors can't save everybody.

Eventually, anger and blame give way to a state of depression. Sometimes this state may continue for a very long while, but it shouldn't last for years. Grieving is, in fact, quite a dangerous emotion. There is a death rate associated with it. Living alone does nothing for someone's health. Nor does loneliness and an ensuing sense of rejection that is often felt by the bereaved – even if the unfortunate deceased had no desire to leave his or her family.

In the first week after a death, the expected mortality rate of a spouse doubles. Often these deaths are from heart attacks. More than any heroine in a Victorian novel, bereaved spouses are likely to die of a broken heart. After this first week, the mortality rate falls, but even after three months it is forty-eight percent greater in bereaved men than it was before the death; in women, just over twenty percent greater. After a death of a spouse, the death rate for a widow or widower doesn't return to that expected for their age and social class for ten years.

The third stage of grief, and the end of obvious grieving, is known as the phase of acceptance. In this phase, the deceased is still loved and missed, but not to the extent that whoever has been left behind can't take up their old life again. In older people – those over sixty-five – the problem of loneliness compounds grief and adds to the stress. Sixty percent of people over seventy-five say they are lonely. More than a third of the people living alone say that they are depressed, and fifty percent of those who are poor and alone admit to the same emotion. Despite this, most people want to retain their independence.

Tips for overcoming bereavement

These are very similar to those who are overcoming the effects of divorce (see page 102), except that there is more to be said in favour of widows uniting against the world than there is for divorced people seeking each other's company.

1 Don't suddenly feel you have all your departed spouse's responsibilities upon your shoulders. You can't do everything, and certainly you can't do everything at once. Use professional advisors: accountants, solicitors, etc.

2 Clubs may be helpful. Some bereavement organizations may sound dreary, but they do serve a useful purpose for the more elderly widow or widower.

3 Remember that the various stages of grief are universal. You are not alone and, sooner or later, everyone experiences them. The different stages vary in intensity but the time at which people move from one stage to another differs.

4 If irretrievably stuck in one phase (sometimes blame or anger but more often depression), talk to your doctor. Treatment is available, but it is a difficult decision to separate normal sadness from abnormal depression.

5 Some find grief counsellors useful. They encourage people to admit anxieties, worries, regrets and guilt. Most of these sentiments are unfounded and exaggerated, but they represent true concerns – and therefore stress factors.

6 Create a structure for your life. Get up, clean the house, do the shopping, the laundry, have regular visits. Eat out, however cheaply, and continue to go to the theatre or cinema and carry on with your interests and charity work.

7 Don't allow yourself to look scruffy. Take the same pride in your appearance as you did when your spouse was alive. 'Widow's weeds', as they were known, are described in the dictionary as being an archaic term, but the paucity of pensions is giving it a new reality.

8 Remember that it is very often more difficult to entertain a single person than a married couple. If the invitations fall off, it is not a personal slight; rather it is an example, however unfeeling, of a social truth.

9 Don't make any immediate decisions about moving. Everybody is sad or depressed after a death. Let the mood settle before doing any more than discussing future changes. Never make important decisions when feeling depressed.

10 If you do move, balance the advantages of being near sons, daughters or siblings against the disadvantages of moving away from old friends and familiar, hallowed surroundings. Remember that children are forever being posted to other parts of the world. It is easy to end up in a new district knowing no one.

Divorce

As Holmes and Rahe described, different events will be bound to cause some stress. There has never yet been a divorce, whatever the participants in it may say, that doesn't cause some stress to one or other partner. Usually there is stress not only for the two principal actors in the drama, but also for all those with cameo roles. Divorce and death produce the same reactions because they both occasion loss.

In both instances, however difficult life was before the separation, there is a grief response. In the grief response, as described in earlier pages, the initial reaction is one of disbelief; just as many people are unable to admit that a loved one has died, and may go on behaving as if he or she were still alive, so after a divorce they can't believe that their erstwhile husband or wife has left them.

After this is accepted, there is a realization that their lives will never be the same again, as many aspects of it will inevitably have been changed. In time feelings of disbelief are replaced by blame and anger. The man or woman who was once perfect is now an absolute monster. If or when this phase of the grief response has moved on to the next – depression and self-pity – recovery is starting. Hopeless depression should only last for a few months before becoming bearable. Thereafter there should be an acceptance of the situation and a new and different life can start to be lived.

At any stage, the process may become stuck. There are people who are still resentful, angry and bitter years after a divorce. Others will become stuck in the depressed phase. This is easier to treat, and the time when treatment is required has to be carefully judged.

In the past it was always considered that the man had it easy after a divorce had occurred. He had his job, his interests, perhaps a new, younger woman, whereas the wife was left lonely, miserable and bereft. Research shows that this was never the whole story. Many men were torn between two people and had overwhelming guilt. They were poor and having to keep two households, and they missed all the day-to-day rituals and mundane activities to which they had become accustomed over the years they had been with their first partner.

Now courts tend to favour the women involved. They have the children, they often have the family home, they have their share of the pension, they don't have to pay for the children's upbringing and often have a lump sum for themselves. The truth is that Holmes and Rahe were right to put divorce next to death in the scale of life's disasters. Nobody is going to come out unscathed.

'You stay right there while I go and get a divorce...'

How the stress of divorce can be reduced

1 Maintain friendships. Friends tend to owe greater allegiance to one partner than the other. Everyone hopes friends will continue to be friends of both, but it doesn't often happen. The divorcing pair should decide how friends are likely to divide and do their best to see that there is a semblance of equality in the division.

2 As soon as possible, start making new friends. You could join singles' clubs and organizations that cater for the divorced, but it's far better to join clubs that cater for your interests, whatever they might be: political, musical, literary, sporting, community-based, etc. Divorced people may have too much in common. It is good to learn someone else has experienced the same problems, but your new life should be based on different expectations.

4 Make sure there is structure to your day. Don't just lie in bed; get up, prepare breakfast and find new interests.

5 Dress as carefully as you did before.

6 Always be polite – however much you're tempted otherwise – about your vanished partner to your children.

7 Never be rude about your former partner's new boy-friends, girlfriends or children.

8 Don't use your children in a complicated game of chess. Like pawns, they can be easily sacrificed forever.

9 Make certain that your surroundings as well as your personal appearance are maintained.

Moving on

When women leave men, the likelihood – no more than that – of a good post-divorce relationship is greater. When a man leaves a woman, post-divorce friendship is rare. If either the man or the woman later has a new partner, or even if they had another partner while still married, don't be inquisitive about it or object. Accept it. Understand that divorce, even if it was at your instigation, represents a bereavement, for there's always an associated loss. It is accompanied by both anger and a sense of failure.

It may be necessary to move. Whether you care to recreate your earlier environment or continue with the old one is up to you. Don't let anyone try to influence you. This is *your* house – not your parents', and not your former partner's.

When your social life recovers and other partners are in the offing, it is worth considering what it is that makes for a successful relationship. People writing a generation ago devised rules for reducing the stress of marriage or long-term partnerships. Their rules are no longer directly translatable into modern life, but they can be paraphrased and enlarged upon so that they fit twenty-first-century circumstances.

The main principle applies equally today. It is that opposites may get on very well at parties, they may have terrific affairs, but they don't make the best long-term partnerships. A sound marriage is not one in which two people, however compatible in bed, are fighting like a couple of Rottweilers for the rest of the time. Rather it is one in which both parties feel totally comfortable with each other. Their relationship is without stress. The number of patients is legion who have said to me that, as much as they are attracted to somebody else, they could never leave their husband or wife because they feel so at ease with them. Where there is tension, there is stress.

Rules for a stress-free relationship

1 Look for your partner from within your group of existing friends or from the place where you either live or work. Marriage will then not be such a wrench.

2 Choose your future mate from a similar background to your own. You will then share the same prejudices, however good or bad.

3 Avoid a marriage or long-term relationship that produces serious conflict as a result of differing religious or political views.

4 Share the same sense of what is important: preferably a sense of humour and certainly the same opinion as to what is too sacred to be laughed at.

5 Make certain that you are in agreement as to whether you want children, and if so, how you feel they should be educated and brought up.

6 You don't both have to have a first-class honours degree. However, marry someone who will understand what you are thinking, even if they wouldn't have had the intellect for those thoughts themselves.

7 Research carried out for one of the country's major organizations showed that the closer the nature of one partner's employment was to the other's, the happier they were.

A tale of divorce

Courage is finite, as Lord Moran, famous physician and medical teacher, also Churchill's doctor, said about soldiers in battle. Everybody has their breaking point. As with courage in facing the vicissitudes of war – the shelling, the bullets, the deprivation and discomfort – so with stress. Even the most detached, even emotionally blunted, will, if the load is too great, crumble beneath it. As to be expected, when cracks start to appear in someone's behaviour or health, where they show will not be by chance. Some people, brought up in a free-and-easy dysfunctional household, might take another divorce in a family riven by divorces with no more than a shrug of the shoulders, and possibly a couple of stiff whiskies to settle the nerves.

Just such a family were the Jameses. Peter James was a successful businessman, so successful that he had bought a late Georgian house surrounded by parkland. He lavished money on its interior so that every room looked like a film set for a 1950s' library. No antique dealer missed a call from Mr James. As with the decorating, so with the staff. Charles, a traditional English butler, was installed. Mr James became an important local figure. Since he was prepared to contribute heavily to the political party he had predicted would win and was as good at assessing political odds as he was predicting City prices, Mr James became Sir Peter James.

All was going well, except that Lady James was rather bored. Lady James, tiring of the view from the terrace and of watching the farmers' cattle grazing in the parkland, spent an increasing amount of time in their London flat.

One Saturday afternoon, after the Jameses had settled down to tea, the telephone rang. Charles came in as silently and respectfully as he always did. 'Sir Peter,' he said, 'it is a call from Chattock and Wiley.' Sir Peter left, came back into the room and said, 'Amaryllis, it's really for you.' His wife went off to the telephone, came back and said, 'Old Wiley tells me you're divorcing me.' 'Yes', said Sir Peter, 'I thought it was for the best.' No more was said. They finished their tea, went out for dinner and the matter wasn't discussed again until after the weekend.

They had several more months of a superficially happy marriage, but separated before the grouse season. They thought the situation might be too difficult for guests they didn't know well, although at home in Dorset, where everyone knew them, life continued as before. Once separated, Amaryllis became happily ensconced with her lover in London. Later, Peter's friends found out that he had had a girlfriend for years. Despite the efforts of Chattock and Wiley (or perhaps because of them), cracks later appeared in their relationship and within a couple of years they were only on Christmas-card terms.

Moving house

Sometimes before marriage but usually within a year or two afterwards, it will become necessary to move house. Moving house figures on the Holmes and Rahe list of stressful life situations. The degree of stress associated with it depends on the size of your income, the amount of time you have to organize it and the sense of loss if you have to move away from your accustomed area and friends. Some problems, however, are universal.

If you are unable to complete major works before you move, or if you are one of those people who enjoy DIY and flatter yourself that you are a good amateur electrician, builder or plumber, try and reduce the stress for the rest of the household. Few people haven't been driven by exigency to move into an uncompleted house. Removers' boxes, dirty, dusty furniture and broken pictures will lie around for months. As in every aspect of life, stress is always reduced if you are realistic about your abilities, know when to delegate and can list the jobs that need doing in order of importance and urgency.

Tips for moving house

1 If your income will stand it, arrange for professional builders, electricians and plumbers to do the work necessary to modernize your new house, or to adapt it to suit your idiosyncrasies and put your stamp on the property before you move.

2 It is much better to complete any major works and decoration before you move. The only stress then will be re-establishing yourself in a new neighbourhood.

3 Label your furniture in your existing house with the name of the room that it is going to in the next house. If you don't, and you think that you can stand in the hall of your new house and direct the removal men, you've got it wrong, and chaos will be the result.

4 Don't do your own packing, and negotiate a deal with the removal firm for the unpacking. The days when unpacking was included in the contract have passed.

5 If you have books, make certain that they are packed as they are taken out of the shelves and not in just any order. It will save you days of work later if they are packed as they come out of the shelves rather than at the whim of the removal men. They simply want to pack their tea-chests neatly.

6 If you have a relatively stress-free move (no move is entirely stress-free) and are becoming progressively less stressed, the principal tension will be experienced when attempting to establish local links in your new place of residence.

7 The above may be comparatively easy if at least one person is working or if there are children at school. Either place (of employment or school) provides an initial point of contact in a new district. If not, then join local community organizations.

Tips for the DIY expert

If you are a DIY enthusiast, here are a few tips to follow if you want to avoid divorce and having to face changing your wife or husband as well as your house.

1 Aim to finish the kitchen, one living room, the bedroom and the bathroom as soon as possible; the rest can wait. So long as there is somewhere to seek sanctuary, to sleep, cook and wash, all may be well.

2 Pawn the engagement ring if need be, but obtain a professional team to finish at least this basic living unit.

3 Don't overestimate your do-it-yourself ability. Don't be over-adventurous. DIY magazines, books and television programmes can be seductively misleading. It is *always* more difficult than it looks.

4 Your partner may underestimate your skill with the Black & Decker, and won't believe that you have a Churchillian ability to lay bricks. Unfortunately, most men are almost as unwilling to admit that they are not very good with a saw as they are to confess that they are bad drivers. Be realistic.

5 Always budget for repairs – not only for the cash outlay, but for the time it will take. This will be much longer than you think, and the materials may cost more than anticipated.

6 Take out insurance. Make certain that your personal insurance covers you against accidents that might injure others, yourself and property. Most DIY-related accidents occur when the DIY-er is tired after a day at work.

7 Have the occasional break from being a navvy or bricklayer.

Noisy neighbours

Of all the hazards that must be avoided when moving house, that of noisy neighbours is near the top of the list of potential stress factors. After a day at work, peace and quiet, preferably both indoors and out, are essential. For this reason, visits to the planning office, chats with potential neighbours, a study of local papers and a rigorous insistence that all the questions are fully answered on the estate agent's questionnaire are essential. Even so, people can get caught out.

The following is a case in point. The Tumbledown Pub ('Always as quiet as the grave, doctor,') celebrated the arrival of one of its new neighbours by applying for planning permission and the appropriate licences to turn itself into a nightclub. The comfortable country house nearby – Edwardian, sound, established – was due to be sold the following week. Contracts had been delivered and deposits had been paid, but the vendor hadn't yet signed his contract.

The night before the contracts were due to be exchanged, caravan-dwellers moved into the field next door. The buyers immediately withdrew, leaving the owners with an unsaleable house. In this kind of situation, a good lawyer is expensive, but essential. Never hope for the best and don't try negotiating yourself; it will only increase their noise, double your stress and halve the likelihood of a happy outcome.

Two court cases later, and legal expenditure equivalent to that of a good middle-grade car, planning permission for change of use was justifiably refused, as was the request for an extension of the licence until 2 o'clock in the morning. The caravans, however, are still in the field of the house nearby, and its owners are now the worried, stressed possessors of two houses, one of which is still unsaleable. Meanwhile, the lawyers grow richer.

Holidays

The Holmes and Rahe scale of life-changing events (see pages 88–89) accords few points to holidays. This may well be a reflection of life as it was fifty years ago. Yet I know from discussing the year with patients at their annual medical that the success or failure of a holiday figures much higher in their dreams and hopes than would be supposed by reading the Holmes and Rahe table. As work has become more demanding, as paternalism and the concept of a two-way loyalty of employer to employee for a working life has faded, and as hours have lengthened without a corresponding increase in the sense of achievement, the importance of a holiday has increased.

If a respite from the commuting rat race has been looked forward to for weeks or months – perhaps even for the whole year – and it is then spoilt, then those who had hoped to enjoy an oasis in the desert that their lives have become may develop a sense of failure.

To further complicate matters, modern holidays serve different purposes, depending on whether a person is married or unmarried, partnered or single, with or without children. The larger the family unit, whatever the nature of the link or commitment to each other, the greater is the chance of disaster, because the more difficult it is for everyone to have their expectations satisfied.

'Annabel, go to your suite!'

Holidays and the single traveller

The choice of companion or group for the unmarried holiday-goer is all-important. Just making this decision can cause stress long before the holiday starts.

The following questions reflect the type of decisions that face singles when deciding on holidays.

1 Will my usual group of friends really want me to go on holiday with them?

2 Is it a good idea to go away with my current boy- or girlfriend once again, or should I try and broaden my life?

3 Can I really afford the destination the others have already chosen?

4 Can I afford to take the time off?

5 And do I really want to go to Miami?

6 Does the rest of the party have the same holiday ideas as I do?

Holidays for those in long-term relationships

If you think that the problems single people face when selecting holiday destination seem almost insurmountable, then consider how much greater they are for some couples. The two people in question may well have been attracted to each other and married one another for qualities that don't include sharing holiday interests, but any differences may be lost in the hurly-burly of everyday life. Once on holiday, however, being shut away together in a three-star hotel bedroom while separated from all the comforts of home life does nothing to improve an already strained relationship.

Some married pairs try to overcome this problem by always going away as part of the group. The groupings are always interesting. Yet even here, there can be pratfalls. Very often, the habitual holiday groups contain one or two people who, for years, have rather admired other people's wives or husbands or long-term partners, and the annual holiday has been an opportunity to enjoy their company – usually innocently. The tensions any jealousy can create for their other halves, however, can be considerable.

Once there is a family, finding a holiday that will suit everyone becomes even more difficult. All is well when the children are small – provided that they don't become ill, sleepless, irritable and homesick. Difficulties begin to arise when they reach the later teenage years. There is not only the question as to whether they will enjoy a holiday with their parents, but they may also be worried about keeping up with the Joneses at school or university. Your week in Corfu may seem dull compared to the visits to exotic destinations enjoyed by your teenagers' contemporaries.

Tips for stress-free holidays

1 Plan the holiday with as much care as the generals planned D-Day.

2 Choose a destination that is easy to reach. If you are already worn out, why plan a holiday in the Andes? If you spend your life driving around the country as a sales director, don't drive an extra two or three thousand miles in your three weeks away.

4 Find a reliable tour operator or travel agent. Later, you may feel enraged when you hear how someone has booked the same holiday off the internet and had a wonderful time for half the price, but there are others whose economy has left them in an unfinished hotel with no air-conditioning. Don't risk it.

5 Get to the airport on time. Make due allowances for unexpected events, before or at the airport. Parking invariably takes longer than is supposed.

6 Insure yourself.

7 Get injections before you go. Everyone travelling overseas should be protected against Hepatitis A; if young and sexually adventurous, also Hepatitis B. You should also be immunized against polio, and be up-to-date with anti-tetanus and anti-typhoid jabs.

8 Take your usual medicines along, such as those for tummy upsets, coughs, stings and bites. An antibiotic cream is often useful. If you're prone to any disease or have a chronic complaint, pack more of your medication than is necessary in case your return is delayed.

*'It's hard enough keeping my eye
out for the police without your comments, Doris!'*

Entertaining

For years, advertisements on television set an impossibly high standard for social entertaining, implanting false expectations of the fun and jollity that should be within the grasp of those who attend dinner parties, race meetings, dances, evenings in the pub and boisterous gatherings at the local yacht club. It wasn't just the guests who were so socially adept that every event had a Hollywood atmosphere of sophisticated elegance; the hosts and hostesses were equally competent and skilled. This, of course, was all nonsense – merely the advertising world's vision of success that would help to sell the products they were plugging. In reality, social occasions are fraught with tensions. Not everyone is feeling totally at ease; many are socially fearful, others are socially phobic and wish that they were a hundred miles away from the occasion.

To be successful, modern hosts and hostesses shouldn't be too ambitious. If giving the party themselves without much or any help, they should remember they only have a limited amount of time. The food shouldn't be planned so as to rival Gordon Ramsay's efforts at Claridges; the table doesn't have to be set like a state function at Buckingham Palace. Have confidence and be realistic. Your friends are coming to see *you* – or if not you, your other guests. The table may look superb when they first come into the dining room, but in no time those eating at it will have spoilt it just as thoroughly as the first footsteps ruin a snowfall. Food should be straightforward; there's no competition for the best and most complex meal; after all, the food and wine at a dinner party is no more than the oil in the social machine that turns the wheels. Never be ashamed, if you are both working and you have no domestic help, of serving something from Marks & Spencer. Your guests will love it – and you will be less stressed.

'I almost died at your pronunciation of "macho"!'

How to have a stress-free dinner party

1 Prepare as much of the meal as possible in advance.

2 Set the table the day before.

3 Take time to sort out the most agreeable seating arrangement. Try to avoid potentially quarrelsome or competitive pairings. Two generals together will have a good talk if they meet professionally and get along well together. On domestic social occasions, however, they are likely to be competitive. Likewise, although striving politicians or successful surgeons have much in common, their greatest similarity at your dinner table will be an equally savage competitive spirit so that each will want to be the authority on the same subject.

4 Take trouble over the drinks. The secret is to make certain that everyone has enough to become slightly less inhibited, but no one should have so much that they become drunk or even so uninhibited that an animated dinner-party flirtation crosses the barrier and has serious intention. A couple of drinks before dinner will be necessary in any case.

5 A dinner party seems more festive if there are at least two different wines. People will drink less of a really good wine than if they think they are enjoying a table wine for quaffing.

6 Be careful when dispensing after-dinner drinks. And never press them on anyone.

7 Don't accept too much help. Guests feel guilty about sitting down while hosts do the work. One waiter may be helpful, but the evening may be ruined if the whole room is buzzing about like bees around a beehive.

8 However tired you are, try to wash up after the guests have gone home. There's nothing more depressing than dirty plates the following morning.

'I'd love to watch the Queen, dear,
but she has domestic help.'

Driving

Research in the 1970s among a predominantly male, middle-class group of people showed that driving more than a certain amount every year (at that time 12,000 miles) became a risk factor for diseases usually associated with stress. Since then, motorways have become much more widespread and the stress of driving has lessened in many respects – despite the tailbacks.

Not every aspect of driving is stressful. Driving alone is an opportunity for uninterrupted thinking time. There is a sense of freedom from both professional and domestic worries. If the advent of the motorway network has made the mechanics of driving easier, however, the advent of the mobile telephone has reduced the isolation that can enjoyably be experienced in the car.

Stress is reduced if a careful timetable is worked out. The timetable should allow for a leisurely drive. Too many drivers, especially those with Type A personalities, compete against the clock. The Redbridge roundabout must be reached within three-quarters of an hour, Stanstead Airport within an hour and a half, Mildenhall within two hours and Norwich within two hours fifty minutes. It's a good day when an hour or so can be clipped off the whole journey.

The motivation that prompts competition against time is quite different from competitive driving against other drivers, but even so, it is stress-inducing. The dangerous competitor on the road who competes against other drivers is stressed even before he gets into his suped-up Mini Cooper or white van. It is said that aggressive, competitive driving on the roads is a sign of stress caused either by sexual, racial or social feelings of inferiority. Whether or not this is true, competitive driving certainly adds to the tension felt by other drivers.

Here are a few basic questions that reveal signs of increasing stress and rising tension that may be caused by life on the road.

1 How often in the last month have you had a near-miss? Even though the potential accident wouldn't have been your fault, the number of near-misses increases as stress in life rises.

2 Are you more impatient when driving than elsewhere?

3 Are your response times ever increased because you are thinking about all those terrible problems in the office or home?

4 Do you find that the number of people hooting at you as you drive through a built-up area is increasing?

5 Obviously you never suffer from road rage, but do you find that you are showing naturally understandable irritation about other road users' driving more than you used to?

6 Are you more easily distracted by passengers so that their chatter is beginning to inhibit your ability to negotiate difficult road conditions?

Rules for stress-free driving

1 Plan your journey so there is plenty of time for it.

2 Have a quick kip if you feel tired.

3 Those who are liable to and frequently feel sleepy should see their doctor. There are now pills available – Provigil – that are useful for the hyper-somnolent.

4 Never drive if the night before has been disrupted and short. A conservative estimate is that one in five of motorway accidents are caused by drivers falling asleep.

5 Remember that experiments that have shown that it is as unsafe to drive with a heavy cold, or even when sickening for some infection as it is for the normally built person to drive with the maximum allowable alcohol blood level. Special care is needed if the driver is feeling unwell.

6 Use the train if the week has been too busy, or there has been a great deal of driving during it.

7 Don't drive to a holiday destination if it is hundreds of miles away. Better to fly and hire a car on arriving.

8 Children may make unhappy and disruptive passengers. This is one of the times when discipline has to be firm. There are few families who can't remember

accidents or near-accidents because their children were fighting like obstreperous puppies in the back seat.

9 Road rage is an unfortunate term as it implies an understandable condition that is not the driver's fault. It causes a great deal of stress to the object of the rage. People who suffer from road rage are disturbed. The variety of psychiatric or psychological problems which may make them liable to road rage are legion. Even so, in many cases the aggressor has psychopathic features. These drivers, absurdly enraged by some minor incident or inconvenience, can't tolerate being frustrated; they are unduly sensitive without possessing a well-developed conscience or sense of responsibility, and they are impulsive and lack self-control.

10 Of all the absurd accoutrements of modern life that may be responsible for financial stress, a car seems to be the most unnecessary. The car has become a symbol of social and sexual potency. It is now a hallmark of temporal success rather than a means for travelling in reasonable comfort and safety without being so dilapidated that its limitations are stress-making. To avoid stress, choose a car that starts, doesn't break down and is capable of cruising without discomfort at the usual motorway speeds. Far better to get a good second-hand car than to suffer penury as a result of competing with colleagues and neighbours.

Telephones

Recent research has shown that the most stressful aspect of domestic and social life is the telephone. The markers of stress – blood pressure, hormonal changes, etc – are increased more by telephones ringing repeatedly while trying to work than by any other aspect of office or home life.

People are now as much shackled electronically by their mobile telephone and pager as is any third-ranking crook who is the subject of some magisterial device. There is no escaping the mobile telephone. It removes privacy and infringes independence, it irritates those who are not making or receiving the calls, and in general, it is one of the most stress-creating machines of twenty-first-century life.

'Tuesday at 4.30 any good for you?'

Tips on telephones

1 Be firm about telephone use. If it wouldn't have been essential ten years ago to be in telephonic communication with the world, turn the mobile telephone off.

2 Arrange the office telephone system so that it doesn't interrupt meetings or times when careful thought is needed. Even though secretaries are almost a feature of the past, it is essential to have telephone calls screened. It is impossible to concentrate on an important problem if the bank manager telephones in the middle of the discussion to sort it out.

3 When tired, it is easy to ramble on the telephone; older people may find that their ability to create neatly turned sentences disappears. Make notes before a telephone call about what you are going to say and always make notes in a book about what the other person has said.

4 If there is an important family occasion, even Sunday lunch, switch on the answerphone.

6 Remember to switch mobile telephones off in public places; it will save angry glances. Never have a long conversation in a public place; go out into the road (if it's a reasonably safe area) or hide in the lavatory, but don't irritate your colleagues or friends.

7 Persuade family members to leave telephone numbers when they travel abroad to save anxious moments.

Weddings

Before people even start to consider the stress of marriage, there is the stress of getting married. Marriage is stressful, but no aspect of it comes close to the stress produced by the wedding and the preparations that go into it.

The first decision that needs to be made is whether the marriage is a celebration of the union of two families and for all generations, or whether it is a party for the bride and bridegroom, together with their select friends. If the latter, there will be countless old friends on both sides who will feel alienated and left out. They will cause trouble for years.

A word about families

In addition to all the other problems that surround a wedding, there are a few basic considerations that apply to all family gatherings, whether they are Christmas parties, weddings, christenings or funerals. Having similar DNA isn't enough to ensure that everyone at the wedding will gel. Families, like any other group, are rent asunder by jealousies or animosities that would have been forgotten decades earlier if the people involved had been strangers. The reason weddings can be particularly stressful is because they are composed of a heady cocktail that is a mixture of the tensions, prejudices and ambitions of two different families.

Furthermore, all generations are, or should be, present. For this reason, no one will know everyone, and many will feel lonely and isolated. Some of the latter may drink too much, and that may add to the difficulties.

'Our marriage is very stressful. If it weren't for the sex, I'd leave him!'

Having said this, weddings *can* (and should) be fun. The consequences of a good wedding may last a lifetime, but this will occur only if the event has been well-planned. Brevity is a virtue in a wedding that is too often overlooked. The easiest weddings to organize are those at which the ceremony takes place in the late afternoon: the four-o'clock slot. The reception that follows then doubles as a pre-dinner drinks party. Dinner over, the aged are free to retire, while all those who regard weddings as a party for the bride and bridegroom can stay on and happily dance the night away.

How to avoid wedding stress

1 Make a budget.

2 Decide who is going to pay for what. The days when the bride's family paid for the lot are passing – if they haven't already done so. Try to find a compromise acceptable to both parties.

3 Agree between the families on the type and details of the wedding. Prepare lists of potential guests, but don't insist that these should be categorized such as 'family only', 'second cousins don't count as family', etc.

4 As in any important lifetime event, planning is the key to success and less stress. Some of the most successful weddings I've attended have been planned down to the last penny and the last five minutes (if not seconds).

5 Both families need to be involved in this planning.

6 Never allow the planning and the budget to spoil the occasion on the day. A disaster or two is to be expected. Funds should have been laid aside to pay for any costs that will undoubtedly be necessary to correct these unforeseen circumstances.

7

Stress at work

The stress interface

Sources of stress have to be divided between those derived from home life or from the office. Wherever the stress originates, there is a common factor. It is the relationship between other people, whether at home or in the office, that causes it. Research carried out in the early 1970s added another dimension to this fact. By studying heart rate and rhythm with a twenty-four-hour monitor, by taking serial blood tests to estimate levels of the stress hormones, and by studying the incidence of angina and even heart attacks, these studies showed that the most stressful periods in any day were at the interface between home and office, and office and home.

Managing the transition

Bill Atkins was a banker who worked in the plushest of plush offices in the West End of London. Whereas all his equals were driven to work every day by a liveried chauffeur in a Daimler, he pedalled to work on a bicycle. The journey took about half an hour. Frequently he was soaking wet; at other times of the year he was running with sweat. When asked why he did this, he said that he could only tell his doctor the true reason. To everybody else he pretended it was because he wanted the exercise and to keep fit.

The real reason was something quite different. When at home, his wife – a good if not tactful woman – disturbed his thoughts as he attempted to marshall them for a hard day at work. The bicycling distracted him; he had a simple repetitive job that took his mind off his wife's thousand and one anxieties. Once at work, he had laid on a bathroom in the office and he soaked in the bath while he recovered. Having had his bath he could face

*'Moments like this take all the stress
out of commuting.'*

the world and the finances of his district. He then went to his office, had a cup of coffee before he saw his first client and read the City pages.

The return journey home was the same in reverse. He dressed up in his cycling clothes, walked in through the door, shouted a greeting to wife and family and disappeared to the bathroom. Recovered, he could face stories of the fishmonger who had forgotten the order, the plumber who had failed to find the leak and made a mess and the telephone call from the insurance company who wanted to know when he was going to complete the valuation forms for the following year. He was even able not only to play with his young children, but to enjoy doing so. The bath over, after a glance through the evening paper and a drink, he belonged to his family.

The usual advice, and it is the advice I have given to hundreds of potentially stressed people dividing themselves between two different worlds (home and office, colleagues and family) is that from the moment people wake in the morning their mind, if not their soul, belongs to their boss. Once awake, they are thinking about the day ahead of them, who they are going to see and what they are going to say to them. They are alerting themselves to the possible hazards of the day and preparing themselves for any necessary crisis management. Their thoughts shouldn't be distracted by being asked to remember to buy some lettuces on the way home, to find out how Aunt Marjorie is coping with her new house or not to forget to ask the secretary to book a flight because 'It will only take a few minutes'. So it will. But the need to do it will be a distraction as it weighs down the mind throughout the day. ('Goodness, I mustn't forget those bloody lettuces.')

Once in the office, the potentially stressed worker shouldn't immediately see anyone who might be demanding or pressurizing. Ideally, for the first quarter of an hour, the busy man or woman should read the favourite part of the newspaper, have a cup of coffee and leave the telephone to the secretary. They are re-orientating themselves and completing the process they began when they woke up. They are now an instrument of the organization for which they work – a cog in the wheel – and home with all its worries is behind them until they leave in the evening. The fewer calls from home, the better. Those that are made should be about emergencies, not chats about fourth-form French.

On the way home the worker should start to think about his or her evening with the family. Work is now left behind, and enough discipline must be developed so as not to take work troubles home. The journey helps. Bill Atkins prolonged his commute by cycling. Commuter trains may seem to be the transport organized by the devil, but when they are comfortable and run to time they perform an invaluable function. They give time for the man or woman to re-orientate from office to home.

When the commuter trains are running badly – when there is no seat, when they are cancelled without notice – then they add to the stress and may be the last straw. It is for this reason that any failure of commuting transport has an effect on morale way beyond its importance to someone who isn't either in a hurry to get to work, or has already been frazzled by the work-day. It is too easy to blame the person who calls in for a drink at the White Lion on the way back to the family, but this may be only the way in which someone living in crowded surroundings can have some time to him- or herself while preparing for the evening's role as husband, wife, father or mother.

Stress and the office environment

As work is more easily altered than family life, it is as well to consider the factors that can be changed in the office or workplace to alter the tensions they impose. The easiest part of the environment to change is often the office itself. This is easy enough if you are by yourself, but as in every aspect of working life, the lower someone is in the pecking order, the more they have to put up with other people's opinions, other people's choice of furniture, other people's lighting and other people's temperature. These are only some of the many reasons why it isn't the person at the top who has the coronary but the minions slaving beneath them.

The open-plan office has been welcomed. Whether this welcome has been orchestrated by a management anxious to save money on building costs and refurbishment, and equally keen to keep an eye on their workforce as keenly as any whip man on a slave galley, is an open question. The advantages of the open office have been so trumpeted by human-resource departments that it requires a brave person to challenge the established belief. Yet they have their disadvantages. There is noise: chat, telephones, mobiles, strangers walking past one's 'pod', which is often only separated from a neighbour by a wall of filing cabinets and the occasional plant battling against an alien environment. The wrong lighting, seating and heating can also be a constant source of stress.

Compromise with colleagues

My colleague who shares my offices likes a chilled existence. An early life by the sea has equipped her to withstand a London winter without heat. I like my office at 75˚F; fortunately scarves, shawls and coats provide some sort of compromise. If you are too low down the pecking order, then there is no room for negotiation. I have known offices when otherwise kindly workers will come to blows over the radiators or the air-conditioning.

Office furniture is also important. It is now accepted to make fun of the diagnosis of repetitive strain injury (RSI). The cynical will accept that the tennis player with a different racket, or one who has changed style for whatever reason may develop a tennis elbow. Workmen are allowed a tenosynovitis – an inflamed tendon sheath, so that the tendon no longer slides easily through its glistening walls – but office workers who complain of repetitive strain injury are thought of as neurotic moaners, anxious for time off, and – who knows? – compensation. Yet the condition does indeed exist.

Repetitive strain injuries

It is fascinating to visit the offices of those who have RSI. Sometimes the cause is so simple. A woman deaf in one ear was positioned so that her good ear is up against the window, and her deaf ear is next to her colleagues. She spent her days typing with her head half-twisted round so that she could hear the gossip around her. Once she was given a new desk, the repetitive strain injury and the aches and pains disappeared. In other cases, tiny women have even shorter chairs, whereas giants have monumentally high stools. Lighting is not varied according to the person.

Generally speaking, someone of sixty needs more light to work by than someone of sixteen, but in an office, all the bulbs are the same strength. Some people are light-sensitive; too bright a light and they will be temporarily blinded.

Even more important than the environment in which someone works in is the nature of the organization for which that same someone works. There are few greater privileges in life than the privilege of being able to decide with whom and where you work. For those in the professional classes this is comparatively easy, but even then, crucial decisions will have to be made. For those who are anchored to a particular locality by the mortgage on their house, their children's schools and a husband or wife who is also working locally, they may have to continue to work exactly where they are and as a result, may have to find other means of reducing their stress.

Once in a job, there is only one factor more crucial than the choice of career, and that is the people with whom you are working. There are few ways of life more stressful than that of a new recruit in a first-rate army regiment: cold, wet, bullied, sleepless and drilled for twenty miles a day, and that is on an easy day. Even so, when I went through this training I can honestly say I enjoyed it – such was the companionship and comradeship of my fellow recruits. Since then, I have done several jobs. Most have provided company cars, offices, secretaries and reasonable salaries with good prospects. Despite this, however, it was the stresses and strains of the job, especially if there were any lack of rapport with my colleagues, that determined the stress. The material benefits never managed to compensate for less-than-good working relationships.

Simple ways of stress recovery

Altering your lifestyle to reduce stress, whether derived from the office or home environment, often involves finding other environments where it can, for a time, be forgotten. One of the favoured ways of recovering from the stress of professional life is to pursue games, sport or some other physical activity. When playing squash, golf or tennis, the stressed person is, for the duration of the game, left with no time to ruminate over the columns of figures that represent the company's accounts. While sweating on the tennis court or concentrating on the fairway, the memories of a disastrous deal or the pain experienced by a patient that may herald the end of someone's life will be temporarily forgotten. Concentration on a ball, whether rubber, plastic or leather, gives people an hour or two of respite from the stresses of life.

Lateral promotion

One of the many causes of stress in patients who consult doctors working in industry is the type that is experienced by people who haven't received the recognition and promotion they feel is justified by their qualities. Promotion in any firm always entails a large element of luck. It is sometimes influenced by bad luck, and at other times by sheer vindictiveness or self-interest of more senior people in the organization. Once the chance of promotion has gone, it has frequently gone forever. Those people who, rightly or wrongly, have been deprived of the career they had wanted but are too old or too encumbered to change jobs can often find happiness by being encouraged to succeed in some different field of activity.

This was known in one organization I worked for as 'lateral promotion'. It was encouraged as a form of compensation, but it is a deliberate compensation, not a subconscious one, like the short man who becomes a tyrant, a formerly unattractive woman who becomes promiscuous or a once bullied person who becomes a lunatic driver. Disappointed by their career as a banker, lawyer or accountant, the person who never quite made it may be forever happy as they climb some alternative ladder.

Unfortunately, people can overcompensate when trying to seek status and acceptance through other interests. At its best, their hobby takes over their lives and compensates for lack of success elsewhere. At worst, the man or woman who has always felt put upon because of their appearance may emulate Napoleon and, whether at work or in the community, become a real tyrant. The stressed then becomes the stressor. Bullying is a frequent and potent cause of stress in the workplace as in home life.

Taking on a new job

The first requirement of any new job is a well-defined chain of command and a reasonable immediate boss. Recognizing the potentially good boss is a skill that can make or break a career. The bad boss is slow to praise, quick to blame, unapproachable by those inferior to him, sycophantic to those who are more important, hides his own inability by dividing and ruling so that he never has a workforce united against him and no one quite knows where they stand. Needless to say, his insecurity is such that he never delegates and undermines his own appointees. Whereas the good worker knows that he must divide his time between his home responsibilities and those of the organization, the bad boss expects total commitment. Not for him the kindly best wishes on a birthday, the congratulations on a daughter's marriage or a child's scholarship.

Conversely, the good boss worries about his staff. When I first worked as a doctor for a bank over thirty years ago, all the new employees learnt that the customers came first, the staff second and the profits for the shareholders third. Now short-termism reigns supreme. Bonuses are often the first consideration, profits the second. It is questionable whether the customers or the rank and file of the staff are the least important. The good boss will not only look after his staff but will be equally concerned about the long term-future of the firm on which the staff's future depends. The self-centred boss will regard the firm with no more lasting interest than does a farmer fattening his stock for Christmas. Once Christmas, in the form of a financially advantageous takeover, has arrived, staff and firm may disappear like dew in the morning. This state of uncertainty created by the avaricious chief executive or chairman without human values so undermines morale that tensions and stress are inevitable.

What is death to satisfaction from any job is reporting to more than one boss, each of whom is of equal status within the organization. This causes huge stress, and inevitably the luckless person who has to do it will be drawn into departmental politics. Every day will be stressful. If the employee is in a position to leave, he or she will be well advised to do so. A few years ago, an advertising agency headhunted the boss of an almost equally distinguished public relations company to be its chief executive. There was no way he could have found out that the role of chief executive was so subservient to that of chairman that he had no power – only responsibility. He left.

Some people's work is made untenable because they are given responsibility beyond their experience or ability. In other instances work becomes untenable because qualities and skills are not recognized and their decisions are overruled. If people either have insufficient control to do justice to their capabilities, if they are given inadequate resources, or have insufficient skills to do their jobs, they, too, should move on if they can.

Few people can be at ease with themselves if their skills are either under-utilized or overstretched. There are two other basic requirements in any appointment. Pay must be commensurate with responsibility and equal to that of contemporaries employed in similar positions. It is very easy for a few months – even a year or two – to accept low pay for a fun job. But if, after a time, the workload increases or suffers setbacks and the salary doesn't change, then a low pay-scale will loom much more significantly.

Reasons to move on

In many specialized jobs, and in relatively unstructured industries, the skills of what used to be known as 'man management' – the relationships of managers and those in senior positions to the rank and file – are abysmal. Recognition of a job well done is rarely expressed. Interest in a junior's promotion is usually slight, and if there is interest it may well be to keep the junior in the subservient position where he or she is doing a useful, supportive job rather than allowing them to succeed in their own right. It is a sad commentary of modern corporate life that it is accepted that the surest way to achieve promotion is to become the tail of a comet that appears to be rising within the organization, rather than being recognized by others for one's own worth. All these difficulties will add to the stress of life. Most are beyond the control of the individual. But once others recognize the difficulties, tension is eased. Once the facts of the situation have been teased out, a reasoned decision can be made about whether to stay or move on.

The brave, the tough, those with nothing to lose, no dependents and no school fees to pay can move to a more amenable situation where communication is better, command is structured, and quality is recognized and encouraged. Those who have a family at good schools in the neighbourhood and an affordable mortgage, may have to stay. They should attempt to reorganize the firm. A word of warning: any organization is stressful, even when there are good reasons for it. Even worse, as is often the case, reorganization is made in order to satisfy the ego of the latest person to take command.

In every case I came across in thirty years working as a doctor in commerce, the person delegated to organize the firm's restructuring was thanked profusely, congratulated on its success and within a year or two was replaced. A major change in approach and responsibilities in any organization inevitably involves treading on sensitive toes. The successful reorganizer will have made him- or herself enough professional enemies to guarantee an early demise.

I once asked the chief executive of one company to what he owed his success within that firm. He said there was no doubt about this. He fed his ideas to other people, allowed one of them to put them into practice, waited for him or her to become so unpopular that he would be replaced – and then he took his job. 'Doctor,' he said, 'never be first over the top. They're the people who get shot.'

Another chief executive who had recently taken over the British subsidiary of an American company was severely depressed. Antidepressants only helped to a certain extent. They cheered him up and gave him just enough enthusiasm to keep going. A few months later, when he came to see me, he was much better. He was still taking his tablets but he told me these were no longer so important. He had found out the answer to his stress and depression for himself. He had inherited, as he said, a wonderful and competent team, but they weren't his own; he hadn't selected them. One day he decided to sack the lot. Over the few months since I had last seen him they had all gone. He was as happy as Larry.

In many companies this level of uncertainty and injustice exists. Little wonder, then, when even a decent man (as this man undoubtedly was) can cause such uncertainty in his workforce, that job uncertainty is frequently the cause of unbearable stress. It would be no surprise if, as a result, the affected staff members became irritable, over-emotional, sleepless and even irrational.

'I've had my share of insults, but until now,
nobody has ever said, "Drop dead" !'

'When you've blown out all those candles, you can make a witty little speech.'

8

Stress at home

When stress enters the home front

When people put on business suits, gather the papers and set off for the office, they assume the mantel of the successful wage earner. Whatever may be happening at work, the sufferer of stress is not initially going to disclose it either to his or her spouse or to the rest of the world. Neither men nor women are going to admit impending failure to their workmates or the people they meet for lunch or have a drink with on the way home.

The first aspect of a stressed person's life to crumble, even if the cause of the crumble is stress at work, is likely to be the domestic situation. Once back with the family, the bravado is usually left in the hall with the office coat and briefcase. Not all people stressed at work will immediately want to confide in their spouses, and certainly won't talk about their office problems in the presence of the children. Male or female, they will sit morosely and unsmiling in front of the television set as the words of the newscaster pass unheard over their heads.

The role of the spouse

As soon as the first signs of stress appear, first-aid treatment must be applied. It is the spouse who, sooner or later, has to do this. The treatment is to be a ready listener: one who is questioning and understanding but never judgemental, and neither condemnatory or panicky. The ability to withstand stress, and to pursue a course of action that has a chance of defeating it, may well depend on the choice of a spouse made probably at least ten years earlier and in very different circumstances. Stressed people are not always easy patients. One of the first symptoms they display is that they stop talking, keep their own counsel, forget how to smile and seemingly will never laugh again. They will toss and turn when they go to bed, their sheets will become rucked and their pillows damp with sweat as they wrestle with the troubles of the day.

The problems someone is facing at work may also be made drastically worse if, by coincidence, troubles occur at home at the same time. A comparatively simple incident, such as a minor car accident, can so increase the stress of a difficult job that professional life that was just possible may suddenly become impossible. A person who is already under pressure at work may only have to sort out a simple domestic problem for that request to overload an already heavily laden timetable.

The old rule that no one should ever aim to fight on two fronts is as applicable today to twenty-first-century wage-slaves as it was to Victorian generals. Those who cannot discuss their stress with a spouse should seek the help of their doctor. The doctor will give a non-judgemental opinion and is able to seek the support of the counsellors of the primary care team. Between them, they will be prepared to lend the necessary willing ears.

When talking to the stressed person, either doctor or spouse may be tempted to make suggestions that could cause lasting offence if they came from anyone else. Listeners should not use such a discussion to criticize and to make offensive remarks. However true they may be, no marriage is so sound that it is not weakened by the exchange of cruel home truths. A home is a sanctuary where everyone has the right to expect love and acceptance. Unkind remarks, whether made as the result of anxiety, tiredness or exasperation, will never be forgotten – nor forgiven – even if they are no longer referred to.

There will, however, have to be a full and frank talk about each partner's jobs, the responsibilities they have at home and the time each has available for mutual activities. Many families are riven by an excluding hobby – hence golf widows or men who find that, when they come home, their wives have already left for the bridge party or the reading group. Although nobody wants to spend all their time in the company of one other person, and individual pursuits are part of the recipe for a happy marriage, these pursuits should, nonetheless, never be all-time-consuming.

'Your dog seems to have done a whoopsie in
the utility room, so be careful where
you put your feet.'

Friendships

For those who are married or have a long-term partner, the question about who is the best friend is usually already determined. Very few people are truly self-sufficient, so that those who are single are reliant on good friends. This is especially true with women (and that is not male chauvinism, but the result of careful research) who are reliant on having a few good friends. At least one of these is such a good friend that she can be asked to share all worries and be privy to the most embarrassing confidences. This special friend will understand when the stressed person is upset and learns to detect the true state of affairs, however dramatic and exaggerated the initial account may have been.

Women's friendships are different to those of men in many ways. A study some years ago reached the conclusion that twenty percent of women had close emotional friendships with other women, whereas with men this degree of empathy is rare. However, men who have no male friends to confide in will very probably have a woman, other than a wife or regular partner, to whom they can talk. It may be someone at work; it may be an old colleague or the wife of a male friend. As friendship is such a valuable stress-reliever, efforts should be made to maintain it.

Tips for stress-free friendships

1 Be relaxed. Tension is as destructive to a friendship as weed-killer is to a lawn. The relationship must be mutually rewarding to each person.

2 Friends need to be able to live their own lives. They must never become 'substitute partners', and there is no room for jealousy in a healthy friendship.

3 Very few people are able to keep a secret. Be especially careful to be discreet about your friend's problems. Likewise, never be rude, critical or unkind about your friend. It will get back to him or her, and the friendship will never be the same again, even if all is eventually forgiven.

4 Just as love is supposed to be all-accepting, so should long-standing, firm friendships. Neither person should ever be judgemental.

5 Be honest with each other, by all means. But always be polite and treat one another with respect.

Stress at home in partnerships and marriage

Whether you're a man or a woman, marriage is stressful. It not only involves a change of lifestyle or problems with shared finances, but there is bound to be a marked change in the pattern of living for both people – even if they have lived together before. Somebody else not only has to be considered, but has to be considered as carefully, if not more carefully, than one's own needs. At its simplest, the marital relationship is agreeing on sleeping and eating routines. At its most complex, it is exercising the tact and forbearance necessary to unite two families without being unfair or alienating either set of in-laws. New loyalties have to be established. There needs to be greater loyalty to the recently acquired spouse than to parents and siblings, and it is difficult to achieve this without causing offence.

In the past in many cultures, the new wife moved into her husband's family. Jobs were settled. The boy grew up, and as likely as not he would become a farmer, carpenter or doctor like his father. When qualified and married, he joined his father, and his possibly complaining wife came along, too. There was no option; either she fitted into the family or she was likely to be friendless.

Now, with mobility of labour, the end of most family firms, family trades and professions, the new son-in-law will as likely as not seek employment near his wife's family. It is noticeable that the equivalent of the old music-hall joke about in-laws has changed. The dragon used to be the mother-in-law of the wife who came to visit and complain. Now it is the mother-in-law of the husband who is the visitor and the butt of the jokes.

When the concept of the extended family was all-important, the choice of a partner was not made as a result of a romantic whim but often consciously or subconsciously based on economic considerations. In other parts of the world, this is still considered not only reasonable but essential, just as it had been in the UK in earlier centuries.

Falling in love is a risky business, the results of which, if other circumstances were not propitious, our Victorian ancestors would have thought could be far too uncertain to form a sound foundation for a marriage. Love in those days wasn't despised, however; it was even welcomed – provided that one of the two people concerned could support a wife.

All that has changed. Now love is all, and as a result, many marriages have stresses in them that wouldn't have existed in an earlier era. Money is the modern man's muscle. In primitive times, the woman married the strongest man and thus fared best. Today, the rich are able to buy their way out of trouble. It is no great sociological secret that the most common cause of marital disharmony is financial stringency.

Even in these days when romance rules, marriage must still be approached in a realistic way. Love can have its head, but if stress is to be avoided, the likely pitfalls must be anticipated; to be forewarned is to be forearmed. Over the last seventy years, modern marriage has been evolving, and with it, long-lasting stress. Before the Second World War, enough of the old order was left for marriages to be undertaken for material and economic reasons. The passion may not have reached any great heights, but a comfortable life resulted in many long marriages and a very deep, if not always lustful, relationship.

During the middle of the last century, when the concept that a marriage should be based solely on love had become predominant, the old morality still remained. People hadn't yet become accustomed to living together outside of marriage, discarding unsuccessful partners and living through periods of mini-divorce. These losses are stressful; they excite the standard grief response of loss, but this modern stress is not as devastating as was the case when an old-style marriage was a failure and crumbled after decades of life together.

Those who married in the 1950s and '60s married under the new rules governed by romantic attachment, but nonetheless they didn't have the end-of-century trial period of living together. The moral restrictions on sex were derived from the overriding need to avoid unwanted pregnancies and having children who would be the responsibility of the community and extended family – the latter-day equivalent of the biblical tribe. Once adequate contraception became available and unwanted children were no longer a possibility, the opposition to living together before marriage had nothing to do with considerations of sexual morality. Unfortunately, these two different social issues – whether to have a freer sex life and whether to live together before marriage – have been treated as the same dilemma.

The stress of separating from a live-in partner would be avoided if people still retained their own base whether or not they wanted to spend a few nights a week together. If these two lifestyle decisions could be separated, the distress of 'mini-divorces' that follow periods of cohabitation could be eased. These cause stress, misery and a sense of rejection and failure, as well as grief for the partner who has been dismissed after being found unsuitable when subjected to closer examination.

How to avoid stress in partnerships

Based on my own experience in medical practice involving the care of a predominantly young group of patients, the following steps should. help to prevent some extra-marital stress.

1 Avoid living together. Don't confuse this decision with the decision of whether to have pre-marital sex.

2 Remember that the statistics show that a long period of cohabitation followed by marriage has a higher instance of breakdown and divorce than marriages where the couple have not lived together or, if they have, it has only been for a short time after marriage was already agreed and the date was fixed.

3 Sex is stressful because there is always a judgemental element to it. Comparisons are made. The one aspect of sex in relation to a long-term partnership is whether cohabitation should always be considered or desired once it has become a regular feature of a friendship. The assumption that cohabitation should be the norm if regular sex is taking place is as potentially stressful as an old shotgun marriage.

4 Sex with a married partner has its own particular stresses. Unfortunately, the opinion of the popular press, films and television is that the correct behaviour for a man or woman who falls for a married person is for the married person to become divorced, so that their adultery may be sanctified by re-marriage.

Sex

Just as any change in the appetite for food or drink may give people (and any doctor caring for them) an indication of their mood and the amount of stress they are under, so may variations in a person's libido, or sexual drive, reveal important evidence of tensions and happiness or unhappiness.

If a people who are normally huggable, approachable, and don't find it difficult to establish an easy, if chaste, close relationship with people of the other sex suddenly find that the sexual frisson that oils social life has dried up, it is usually indicative of tensions in their lives – possibly of stress, depression or both. Any change in personality is important, and this applies to sexual personality as well as every other branch of life.

Likewise, if someone is normally rather reticent sexually but suddenly becomes demanding in the bedroom and very possibly promiscuous, then this, too, needs assessment. For the prevention of stress, people not only have to find a pattern of sex that suits them, but also one that is going to be acceptable to the culture of the family and the community to which they belong. One of the definitions of the antisocial personality disorder – the personality type that used to be known in less politically correct days as a psychopath – is that he or she is unable to conform to the social norms of their group and is incapable of sustaining a totally monogamous relationship for more than a year.

The constantly changing partnerships in these disordered lives will inevitably produce stresses and tensions – even in people who are impulsive, seek immediate gratification for all desires, and feel neither guilt nor remorse. The discussions of limiting stress from sexual life have to concentrate on those whose lives do conform more closely to the standard pattern.

Even the most well-adjusted people find the bedroom stressful when they first enter it with a new partner. The greater the vulnerability of their personality, the more they dread judgement, and the new partner is going to judge some of the most intimate aspects of one's anatomy, physiology and psychology. However absurd, the memory of a cruel judgement and a misplaced remark in the bedroom may blight your life forever. Although popular mythology has it that men are the worried ones when it comes to performance, sex can be a source of stress for women, too. Women are sensitive about their figures and can and do compare themselves unfavourably with other women. They feel ashamed of their bodies. They worry about their large or small breasts – or what they perceive to be large or small breasts. They are concerned about their sagging bottoms (sometimes a little-known adverse effect of smoking) or the rolls of fat around their tummies. They are concerned about having thighs shaped like the breeches of a First World War officer.

Little wonder that some want sex with the light out. Women, too, feel less than feminine because – unlike men – they don't routinely have an orgasm on every occasion; many never have one as the result of penile penetration only, but more often as the result of masturbation. They try to hide this guilty secret by faking an orgasm. The only advantage that women have over men in the shame and guilt stakes is that the amount of lubrication they have (the equivalent to the erection) is rather better concealed.

The other advantage men have is that they are more shameless about their bodies. They are concerned about penile size but not much else. They are brazen about their waistband

and beer belly; the concept of cellulite – unscientific as it is – hasn't worried them. Many are indifferent to sweating and even more basic hygiene. Men feel they are being judged on their genitalia. Many a man has been to see me because he feels that his penis is either too small or, very occasionally, too big. The most anxious man who was concerned about his penis being too large had to be admitted immediately to a mental hospital.

Later in the consultation, he had told me how he was so jealous of men with smaller penises, who from his stalking activities he had decided were seemingly having a better sex life than he had; he said that he had been following them and was going to murder one. Incidentally, the physical examination had revealed a penis which, in my opinion, seemed of a very ordinary size.

In fact, size does matter to some women, but only to a very limited extent; other attributes well-removed from the groin, such as eyes, smile or expression are far more important. Rather casual research at a busy clinic some years ago showed that women who had many partners didn't rate the biggest penises as the most desirable; in fact they found very large ones a turn-off. Girth, they thought, was more important than length; as one of the interviewees said, 'What the average woman wants is a good cigar rather than a cigarette, however long.' Surprisingly, an unexpectedly high number of women were interested in the size of a man's testes. I've always used the results of this ad hoc research as one way of reassuring men who are not well-endowed and are concerned about it.

The other problems men have are performance-related. They are concerned lest their erection is inadequate for what is needed, and if having achieved an erection, they are worried in case they lose it too soon – either because they have ejaculated too prematurely or because it has faded. A different anxiety, or perhaps another psychological fear, is experienced by those who suffer from the opposite problem. They can retain their erection but they are unable to ejaculate. In older men, or those who may have had too much alcohol, are taking medication or may have, for instance, diabetes or renal disease, there are some physical reasons why their penile skin has lost its sensitivity – and with it, an easily excited trigger that leads to ejaculation.

The following questions will help detect changes in libido and point to such possible causes as stress or depressive states.

1 Has your libido increased or decreased?

2 Has your mood ever been so low that you feel the only way to lift it is by seeking the support and company of someone of the opposite sex (other than your partner)?

3 Conversely, have you lost all interest in sex? Has your attitude to sex changed, and has the interest you have in it become perfunctory?

If you do decide that there is undue stress in your intimate life, then the next step is discussing the problem. The discussion that needs to reduce any level of bedroom stress and sexual judgement has to take place between two partners. In no other aspect of life is a discussion built on such thin ice. Every phrase has to be thought out, and yet someone's hitherto secret desires have to be conveyed to the partner without mortally offending them.

How to approach an intimate discussion

1 Try to be positive – even if you think that your man's (or woman's) performance, however proud he may be of it, is derisory. For example, find some small aspect of his lovemaking that meets with your approval and starts the conversation by using this as the introduction.

2 Never ever make a humorous reference to either a person's genitalia or performance. Personal remarks are never funny in any context, but in the bedroom they may finish what had been a relationship with a future.

3 Having established that your partner is, if not adept, passably proficient in this particular aspect of sex, ask him or her to use the same talents to do something you would find exciting, but which has never been noticed, although you have been hinting about for months.

4 There is great talk about sharing fantasies. In my clinic, I never found that suggestions along these lines met with a ready acceptance. An easier approach is to buy a copy of one of Nancy Friday's books and use it as an introduction to a joint discussion about fantasies. This will probably uncover anyone's secret desires.

5 Women have often complained to me that not only do men not discuss their fantasies, but they never tell them what they are enjoying as they make love. The reticent approach can be carried too far.

Affairs

Margaret Thatcher, when prime minister and faced with a scandal involving one of her principal ministers, suggested it could well be far more difficult and morally estimable to stay married in order to maintain the family structure than to opt for a quick divorce. She was attacked for this remark, but it was both true and pertinent. The stress of conducting an affair is partly related to time constraints and partly to concealment and deception. All may be fair in love and war, but maintaining a dual life unavoidably based on a series of lies is inevitably demanding and stressful – especially as the time constraints cause trouble with both lover and spouse.

The modern working day doesn't leave enough prime time for the family unit, let alone keeping two men or two women happy. Everyone ends up being disgruntled and feeling that they are losing out. Searching other people's pockets and bags for incriminating bills and tickets, reading their emails, opening their letters and bugging their telephone calls is not the recipe for a stress-free life. Nor is it likely to lessen the tension for someone already torn in two ways by love for two people to have to remember what was said to whom and where some incriminating scrap of paper was placed.

How to avoid stress in an unavoidable affair

1 Remember that, in the final analysis, if the person who is married is not going to divorce, the principal concern has to be to preserve the dignity of the betrayed partner.

2 Any children, even if adolescent, are almost as important. Stress on the family will be greatly reduced if this rule is remembered.

3 Be discreet.

4 Don't expect too much. Demanding exclusivity of an extra-marital partner is one sure way of making a rod to break your own back. Face up to it to the fact that, if you're not ready to commit, you can't expect a similar commitment.

5 Likewise, unmarried lovers, linked to those who are married, have to remember that, so long as their partners remain married, they won't have the time to be satisfactory lovers, as this always involves far more than a few snatched hours in bed.

6 Both partners in an affair are likely to become resentful and feel they are becoming overtaxed. This is another factor that simply must be accepted.

Families and finances

The greatest source of stress in a family is financial. When people first marry, they share not only a bed but a bank account as part of the new, 'great togetherness'. What a mistake! Suddenly they have no privacy; they are unable to by secret presents, and there is no spending, however unwise, that the spouse will not know about. A much better system when starting out is for each partner to keep a private bank account while setting up a new joint account out of which household and family bills will be paid.

Managing debt

The only problem with this scenario, however, is that the stressed person will have to confide in his or her spouse about any outstanding debts. Many a spouse has a huge debt that has been undisclosed. While sorting this out is a matter for the bank manager, and the partner may not even have to know the size of the debt, he or she should know that there is one and that it is being dealt with by the financial experts.

If the debt is a family one, and not on either of the private accounts, of course the exact amount must be known to both parties and the steps taken to deal with it must be agreed. It may mean trading down on the house, re-mortgaging or having some other form of loan, but at least this is a mutual decision; once it has been made, the atmosphere may lighten. It may be that the family finances have received their day-to-day management from the wrong partner and that a handover of power is called for.

Stress and children

Once married, one of the great stresses may be the solicitous or frankly inquisitive questions about the couple's plans concerning children. If childlessness is planned, or even genuinely accepted, then any stress surrounding prying comments should be minimal. In these cases, total honesty will usually stifle any further questions.

In those cases in which childlessness is involuntary, however, even well-intentioned questions and comment can be hugely hurtful and, subsequently, stressful. While the obvious tactic would, again, seem to be being totally honest about the situation, some people can't bring themselves to discuss their own infertility. The best solution if have fertility problems is to seek professional help earlier rather than later. The actual time a patient will be recommended to see a gynaecologist interested in infertility will depend on the woman's age, her previous history and the presence, or otherwise, of any other medical problem.

When to seek help about infertility
Women over thirty-five shouldn't wait for more than six months provided that they have been having regular, repeated sex (it is surprising how often someone who complains of infertility only has intercourse once or twice a month). Younger people could wait a year. Don't regard the doctor's suggestions as criticism. In particular, don't be offended by any suggestion of losing weight, as studies have shown beyond doubt that the fertility of overweight women is greatly reduced.

In the event of being given a timetable to follow so as to have intercourse at the time of maximum fertility, the stress for both the woman – overzealous in her desire to become pregnant – and for her partner – to provide sex on demand, without even the pretence of spontaneous desire on the part of his woman – can be so traumatizing as to be impotence-inducing. As with most aspects of sex, it is much better if it is all regarded in as light-hearted a way as possible.

When children arrive

When a couple is at last 'blessed' with children, other troubles start. Children are hugely rewarding and fun, but their presence is very stressful so long as they are dependent. Most people are naturally anxious to do their best for their children. It reinforces the concept that much of today's stress is the fear of judgement (see page 50), and the more sensitive the person is, the more he or she fears this. There is the certainty that the children's friends are judging the parents, as are their teachers and the neighbours. There may even be a fear that the children are in fact judging their mother's and father's parental skills and other qualities. Likewise, the children grow up with the knowledge that their parents, however much they love them, are anxious that they should 'do well'. This instils performance anxiety in the children.

Just as life is easier if a spouse has a similar intellect and similar interests as his or her partner, so the same principles apply to the relationship between parents and children. The love a parent feels for a child doesn't depend on this. Love conquers all in this case – or so it should. However, the friendship that will develop between parent and child over the years does depend on bonding, and this is greatly eased if parents and children (however old) can play together as well as eat together. If there is a total lack of intellectual interest in the child of a professor, it may well be that the genetic mix has thrown up an unlikely offspring, but his or her different interests inevitably result in little in common between them, other than an assumed parent-child love. This can be stressful for all parties concerned.

When problems arise with children

Children who have medical or academic problems present difficulties which may be understated and denied by some parents. Children can and should be loved for themselves – not for their achievements. Although there isn't a parent in the world who isn't proud of a child's success, parental love should never be dependent on that success.

The surest way of producing trouble within a family is to make fun of a child or to make a joke about his or her achievements or personality – at any time and under any circumstances. Even 'throwaway remarks' which are not recognized as hurtful by a parent can have repercussions for the rest of a child's life. The number of my patients who remember some casual remark from their childhood that has weighed on them for forty or fifty years is extraordinary.

If there is any discord between parents concerning the treatment and upbringing of their children, the best advice is to seek professional help from a good, sympathetic paediatrician. Often a doctor, other than the family doctor, is able to give advice which, if it had come from someone close to the parents, would have caused offence.

Tips for young families

1 Parents are generally kindly. If their child is not as bright and intellectually inquisitive as might have been hoped, they blame it on Great Aunt Susan's genes. It is far more likely that the true cause is the conduct of the delivery and the care the child had at birth. It is pointless to work for the shiniest and fastest car in the street and not to work with equal determination to make certain that your child comes into this world in a way that is going to preserve every grey cell possible.

2 The interval between the children's birth is important. Under two years, and sibling rivalry is very likely to be an issue in the household – very stressful. Much over three years and it will be like having two only children. One of the secrets of family life is having children who can play together peacefully. It is better if there are three children, because then the children become three musketeers who are emotionally interdependent. The stress on the parents is eased.

3 Newborn babies nearly always produce stress. The mother is tired after her pregnancy; she is still recovering from delivery. Newborn babies cry. While this may be music to a grandmother's ears and delight old-fashioned Victorian nannies, for everybody else it produces anxiety and attention. Nature has designed it this way. What is remarkable is how quickly most healthy babies settle into a routine. A word of warning, however: they may not settle into a routine if they sense that their parents are stressed.

4 The sleepless baby or young child can be a problem. Seek expert advice. All that is usually needed is confidence, and talking to an expert may instil this into you. Exclude any physical cause; be firm, follow all the usual rules, and if the child is happy, healthy but merely sleepless, don't worry. I've long since ceased to be surprised to learn that many of the little children I was consulted about because of their lack of sleep at night have turned out to be geniuses.

5 Once a couple has a child, the parents' love should not be divided but rather it should expand to cover all. It is, however, stretched between that for a spouse and that for a child. Likewise, the amount of time available needs to be shared between partner, child and work. Just as it is difficult to have a lover and spouse because of the lack of time so that neither feels well looked after, the same problem arises with children.

6 If only one parent is working, then the mornings, before setting off for work, should be reserved for thoughts about the job. Conversely, after taking time to re-orientate to home life, the evenings and all weekends should be reserved for the family.

7 If two parents are working, then daytime child-carers are essential. They need to be chosen carefully. Many regard your child as a meal ticket: a means of making money. And their love for your child is dependent on his or her good behaviour and ready smile. Yet even good

child-carers can cause stress. The trouble is that the good nanny naturally attracts devotion from a child – a devotion that may seem greater than that currently offered to the parent. It would be unnatural if there wasn't jealousy. This jealousy and the associated stress it causes is the price paid for continuing to work. The consolation is that everyone has a role; the parents' role grows as the child grows, whereas that of the nanny, *au pair* or mother's help diminishes. The important decision to make is whether daytime child-care should be extended into the evenings and even weekends. In some jobs, this is inevitable, and not to have help other than during normal working hours would produce tiredness, irritability and stress.

8 Jealousy, usually neither admitted nor spoken, isn't confined to jealousy for the child-minder. It can extend to visiting grandparents, attentive aunts and boisterous uncles. And it frequently exists between the two sets of in-laws. As parents, your role is to put your child first and to be as scrupulously fair as possible between your own parents and relatives and your spouse's relatives. This jealousy, although common, is absurd. Even the most intrusive in-law disappears after a comparatively short time. Your carefully created regime may be shattered for a day or two, but it is not enough to worry about for more than a second.

9 There may be jealousy between the two parents if one is favoured by the children. Each parent will have his or her day. When children are young, the absentee parent,

whether mother or father, usual has 'treat value' when they are actually there. This is very jealous-making for the parent who has struggled at home looking after them. Be aware of it, and be aware it is happening in hundreds and thousands of families throughout the country. As children grow up, so their needs will change and they will turn to either parent depending on what particular need they have that requires satisfying at that particular moment.

10 Many parents find discipline difficult. It is stressful for everyone to have a battle royal with a child or children. To avoid this stress, decide what matters and ignore everything that doesn't. Does it really matter if a three-year-old has broken a mug or spilt the milk? Does it matter if the child doesn't finish its supper? To make it an issue will only ensure a repeat performance at the next meal, and a worsening in the child's father's angina. Just forget it and ease the stress. The issues that matter are those which affect the health and safety of the child and the rest of the family. Everything else can shrugged off.

11 The over-anxious parent will cause great stress in family life. What do you do about it? Nobody is going to be able to give a parent a new character in his or her twenties or thirties, but it would be worthwhile to seek expert advice. Just realizing that the problem is not the imminent danger to the child but the chronic anxiety state of the parent is a help, as thereafter it can become a family joke – provided the over-anxious parent has insight into his or her condition.

Older children

Parents who are driven crazy by three children under six, four, seven, or whatever the particular household's formula for chaos is, content themselves that once the kids are all of school age and 'beginning to grow up', then all will be well. It won't. Parents invariably worry about their children, and they invariably worry about whether they have done or are doing the best by them, no matter what age the children are.

As all children are different, there is no foolproof recipe for ensuring a smooth relationship. For a variety of reasons, I found myself running a drugs clinic for three or four years in the late 1960s, before drug abuse was put under the control of the psychiatric services. I was struck by the relationship between drug abuse in adolescents and the amount of time their parents, in particular their fathers, could devote to them. I soon realized that it wasn't so much the actual prime time that any particular parent didn't have available for sharing activities at home, but the assumption by the children that the father, or less often the mother, didn't really want to be with them, preferring instead his or her life in the office, overseas business weekends or city council meetings mid-week.

The importance of communication

It is necessary for a parent prevented by work from being an attendant father or mother to say to the children, 'You know that I would far rather be with you than at the meeting, office or whatever, but I have to earn a living.' This helps to keep the family together, and statements of this sort cannot be made too often. Children are insecure, and so just as a woman need to be told that she is loved, so do children – even if they find it embarrassing, even the actual 'L' word is not used. Children will only grow up happy and secure in their own future relationships if they understand that they are loved.

Furthermore, this love must never be thought to be dependent either on good behaviour, good looks, a first-class brain or athletic ability. It has to be unconditional. As children grow older, their worries will increase as they realize that the world is a progressively more competitive place, and that many who want to excel can be ruthless about how they go about it.

Small children – the under-fives – have many of the main characteristics which in later life would be associated with psychopathy; they can be little terrors to each other even though within a few years they will be quiet, decent citizens. Likewise in adolescence, when the hormones start to burgeon, teenagers can be mentally brutal to each other. Sometimes this is associated with jealousy, but at other times it is because they reject and are cruel to those who are weak or different. Whatever the reasons for this difficult behaviour, if children know that they are loved at home, that knowledge will help them to withstand whatever their peer group throws at them.

There are basic rules to bringing up children, but as with all rules, they can often be disobeyed without problems. After all, every family is different, and there are no perfect parents. The main thing to remember is to keep stress – of whatever sort – in check for all concerned.

How to achieve stress-free parenting

1 Family decisions should become 'cabinet decisions' as soon as the children are old enough to understand simple questions. As in the cabinet, everyone can have a say. Parents should show a genuine interest in what the children say, but their decision has to be final.

2 Plan leisure activities. The old cliché about 'families who play together stay together' is true. Joint interests will help the family through the difficult teenage years and lay the foundations for later adult friendships.

3 Be straightforward and honest with your children. Discuss with them, and in front of them, the situation in the Balkans, the problems of one-parent families and the 'druggie' households on the other side of town. Never assume children are too young.

4 Kindly realism rather than liberalism produces happy children. Children should be taught to accept other people's frailties and peculiarities and should learn that it shouldn't make any difference to the way they are approached. On the other hand, they should also learn that, while many desires and feelings are understandable and natural, they often have to be kept in check. Having a realistic, honest appreciation of the motivations of other people in childhood can be life-saving.

5 The children of two types of parents are most likely to appear in the psychiatrist's clinic. The children of both the over-strict disciplinarian and the over-liberal, youth-worshipping adult may be in trouble later. Statistics show that if a happy medium can't be reached, it's better to be over-liberal than over-strict.

6 While it is almost impossible to avoid subconsciously putting pressure on children to do well, try and avoid it.

7 There are types of children-parent relationships which, difficult as it already may be, make a family situation even more fraught. The parent-stepchild relationship is supposed to be the most difficult in the household. Aim for friendship and mutual respect. Unfair as it is, love usually evades these relationships and if there has been an expectation of it, there is disappointment on both sides.

8 The other difficult relationship occurs in one-parent families. Usually some level or degree of emotional co-dependency develops between the parent and the child. The child has to be both child and locum spouse. This burden is too great for many children. They grow up too fast and appear unusually mature. Unfortunately, the experience stays with them and they will always thereafter seek to recreate it by finding mates who are dependent on them. They drift into jobs that utilize or exploit their caring natures but may not be fully stretching their other abilities.

Retirement

Contrary to popular opinion, retirement is one of the most stressful times in life. This is because life is based on a social status that is dependent on what people do for society, and therefore how society regards them. Once retired, the same people who were once contributors to society are sometimes seen by that same society as being parasitic: consuming but not producing. This is nonsense. Retirement is simply payback time; there should be no guilt. These expected fourteen years for men and twenty-three for women have been earned, so what the newly retired should concentrate on is how to enjoy them to the full.

Dealing with 'employment grief'

Strange as it might seem, retirement is another precipitator of grief. As in any grief response, the feelings of gloom and hopelessness are exaggerated in the sufferer's mind. The loss in retirement is not of an individual but of an established way of life, and with it, a feeling that the retired person is no longer contributing to society. Few people like to be parasitic, nor do they welcome losing status. They cannot help but notice that no longer does the retired senior partner or chief executive receive the deference that he still feels his past opinions have earned. He is over-sensitive, feels that he is 'yesterday's man', and fears that all those kind remarks at his retirement party will soon be forgotten – that he will not, in fact, 'always be welcome back in the office'. He (or increasingly, she) knows his fate. The annual pensioner's lunch – if there is one – will soon be the only association with the old firm.

Of course, these feelings on retirement are not universal. Many people have been genuinely looking forward to it and never have a moment to spare in their new busy lives, but I have seen patients who have aged ten years during the first year of retirement. Stripped of their confidence, they look and behave like beaten people. Many retired people have genuine specific worries. Nearly all dread being bored. Most won't be, but these are usually the ones who have prepared for retirement and not just let it creep up on them.

Avoid boredom
To affect the change, plan so that boredom isn't a problem. Try and retire gradually. There is a good case for either retiring very young (say, fifty-five) or very late: say, in the seventies. Those who retire young shouldn't go from a busy, stressful life to doing nothing. If they do, then the boredom that results will be even more stressful than the old job.

You must also retain your independence. After years of having separate daytime lives, a husband and wife shouldn't expect suddenly to do everything together. It is tragic to see the former chief executive reduced to the role of bag-carrier on shopping expeditions or chauffeur to grandchildren's parties.

If young enough, develop new ambitions so that life isn't stripped of purpose, intention and motivation. Work for charity, but remember that charities are changing and a degree of professionalism is now needed. Some people swap the role of chief executive of an important company for being a junior executive in a less important charity. While the wish to be useful is admirable, this can cause life to be even more stressful than it once was. Instead, try to develop a hobby such as birdwatching, playing music, or joining the golf club. This is not the placebo for busy-ness that it sounds; your longevity and your freedom from diseases such as Alzheimer's may depend on the maintenance of a good social life where different people meet regularly in a mutually enjoyable activity.

Give structure to your life. Don't spend half the morning in bed and then make the only gainful activity of the day going out to buy the lettuce for lunch. Get up at the same time as the rest of the world, dress and wash as you did previously, have an organized lunch and dinner. Plan holidays as you would have done if you were still working.

You should also plan your income and expenditure at the beginning of each year, leaving a margin for unexpected events. This has to be detailed, and those who have an appreciable pension should do this with the help of an accountant. As you are no longer in a position to earn more money, you must keep to this rigid schedule. At the same time, the accountant should also make an estimate, no more than that may be possible, as to how income and expenditure will change for the subsequent year so that this may be taken into account. The days when a pension was big enough to leave a person as well-off as when working have passed.

Tips for a stress-free retirement

1 Plan for your retirement on all fronts, financial and otherwise. Don't let it creep up unawares. If possible, retire gradually and use the time gained from partial retirement to rekindle intellectual interests.

2 A hobby that will stretch the intellect and keep diseases such as Alzheimer's at bay may be a good idea. Recent research has shown that the most important single factor in someone's lifestyle that delays the onset of Alzheimer's is the maintenance of an active social life. Choose interests and hobbies that involve social intercourse as well as thought.

3 Visit your family more often. Don't necessarily stay with them, but if you have the means, stay near them.

4 Travel more. Travelling is always difficult when working. Now you can travel freely without any worries.

5 Keep up with your old friends. One of the advantages of retirement is that it is a great leveller. The childhood friend who became a cabinet minister or a general is in a strange position once he has retired. He becomes the equal of the man has not been a great success, and between them, they may find a shared interest.

6 It is essential to beat stress by maintaining a structure to your life. Don't allow standards to slip, as that is the way to social isolation.

9

Lifestyle and stress:
the role of diet and exercise

Diet and stress

It is often easier to change your lifestyle so that stress doesn't occur than it is either to reduce the intensity of any reaction to the stressful life, or to change the approach to the job or home. Although the stress may still be there, it may no longer be so irritating and destructive to the metabolism and cardiovascular system. The obvious place to start in any preventative stress regime is in the realm of diet.

If taken in the wrong quantities, food and drink may not only be symptoms of stress but they may, in fact, create it. Stressed people either eat too much or too little. Those who starve themselves may have a distorted self image; they never realize consciously just how thin they are, and what damage they may be doing to themselves. If depression is a major factor of an anxiety state, the person may well lose weight. The loss of half a stone is always considered significant in medicine. Sufferers of stress-linked eating disorders such as anorexia nervosa and bulimia may lose this amount of weight, although the latter are more likely to be slightly overweight.

Conversely, those people who are both anxious and depressed – and especially when the symptoms of anxiety and feelings of inadequacy predominate – often indulge in comfort eating. This is a vicious circle. Miserable, anxious people eat too much because they are comfort-eating, then become obsessed by food because it relieves these tensions. As the pounds pile on, their already deficient self-image is further eroded. This isn't helped by the fact that, many times a day, those who are overweight are shown pictures of near-anorexic people who they are supposed to emulate but have obviously failed to do so.

In many overweight people, inner unhappiness is concealed beneath a veneer of joviality. This joviality may not only mask the tattered self-image, but it deflects criticism because it tends to make a joke of the person and his or her obesity.

Overeating may, however, be brought on by other causes. It is often a feature of some types of depressive illness, including seasonal affective disorder, also known as SAD, which is triggered largely by a lack of sunlight. In the winter, a small proportion of depressed patients who are suffering from SAD overeat, just as they may oversleep – hence the similarity people notice in the condition to hibernation.

The role of alcohol
Alcohol is another much debated subject. The effect of stress on alcohol intake, like its effect on appetite, varies. In general, the stressed person drinks more. Worn out by a day in front of the computer, it is not surprising that they rush for a couple of mind-numbing drinks once they get away from their place of work. It helps them to unwind. All is well if they keep their daily dose to within reasonable limits. However, very tense and stressed people drink for reassurance or to help them forget their current problems. If going to a party, they may have a couple of snifters before they leave their house, and another quick one as soon as they are at the party. Others drink in order to survive the immediate stresses of work. For example, I once knew a very distinguished statesman who always needed at least two doubles before he went into a meeting. Once there, he needed to be kept topped up, otherwise his natural reticence would hinder his natural eloquence and charm.

There is, as usual, another side to the coin. Just as a depressed or stressed person may feel no pleasure in anyone's company, they may also not want to drink. It is the *change* in someone's drinking pattern that is always of interest to a doctor.

How much is too much?

At present, governmental health guidelines recommend no more than twenty-eight units in a week (spread over seven days – not all at once!) for men and twenty-one units a week for women. The trouble with this recommendation is that anecdotal evidence – and even the evidence of people's own experience – shows that in most cases, this ration is unnecessarily tight. The difficulty official bodies have when recommending safe limits is that not only do they have to avoid rousing the ire of minority groups who have strong moral opinions on alcohol, but they also have to settle on a figure that is so safe that it won't damage either the short, overweight female who can drink only a bit more than her thinner counterparts or the muscular, giant male who can metabolize large amounts of alcohol without risk.

Doctors in public health discussing safe alcohol levels are like engineers who are asked to design a bridge. Just as engineers have to prepare plans so that the heaviest vehicle may cross it safely, so doctors tend to recommend an alcohol dose that could hurt nobody. Thus the engineers' bridge may be absurdly robust for the ordinary family car, and similarly there is evidence that the majority of men don't need to follow the strict limits, for it is unlikely that many will suffer if they drink up to forty-two units in a week. However, there is no denying that the overwhelming majority of people are likely to have serious problems if they drink more than seventy units.

In fact, the safe limit for alcohol consumption varies from person to person. The problem is that if the limits are too strict they are ignored because they are not believed; if too lax, then some people may have trouble. Red wine remains the healthiest alcoholic drink on the market, as grapeskins are utilized fully in its manufacture; as a result, red wines include a larger dose of flavonoids which, as antioxidants, are invaluable to health.

How to recognize dietary symptoms of stress

1 Has your appetite changed?

2 Have you ever been so anxious that you feel you will choke if you have to swallow another mouthful, however delicious the food?

3 A common manifestation of stress is a problem in swallowing created by having a meal with someone you find overpoweringly sexually attractive. Have you ever been unable to eat because of your emotional interest in your companion?

4 Have you noticed when eating that, besides difficulty in swallowing, your saliva has dried up?

5 Have you ever suffered from feelings of nausea or even vomiting in the morning? These symptoms, normally associated with either pregnancy or heavy drinking, may also be caused by stress. Sometimes stress only produces morning nausea; in other cases, the anxious person may actually be sick in the morning. This may be a prominent symptom if a person is unhappy at work.

6 Have you so lost your appetite to the point that you don't even want to eat, even if just with your family? Has the diminished appetite caused a loss of at least half a stone in weight? Severe and persistent loss of appetite is one of the cardinal signs of the depressive illnesses.

7 On the other hand, do you find that your appetite has increased, and that you can no longer resist favourite foods? Have you become a chocoholic? Tense people seek comfort from eating. The extent to which they do so depends on their domestic and professional problems.

8 Are you drinking more or less alcohol than usual? It is a myth that all depressed patients drink more. Some people, when they are depressed, drink to excess; others find that depression removes their desire for a drink. To them, alcohol is associated with jollity and partying and they need the pleasure of convivial company before they want one.

Dieting as stress-relief

Diet is important in the control of stress because it controls weight, and the overweight person becomes stressed. To be overweight is to increase the stress of life. To struggle to lose weight and fail makes the situation worse. All the evidence shows that regular weighing is the first important step in losing weight. Once the true state is accepted, the next step is to find a means of establishing a better pattern of eating. To some extent any diet, providing that it contains fewer calories, and breaks the eating habits of years, is valuable. Part of the strength of the now-popular Atkins diet is that the very strict diet for the first couple of weeks serves to distance the dieter from his or her old ways.

Diets come and go, but the principle remains the same: a slimming diet must reduce someone's calorie intake; if the calorie sums have been correctly totted up, weight will come down. One of the difficulties is that some people put on weight very readily. All doctors have patients who can put on weight even if their diet provides a calorie intake only a fraction of that of the average-sized person. Usually, however, the trick when dieting is to find a weight-reduction plan that doesn't produce hunger but maintains a balanced diet. A balanced diet should not upset the body's chemistry.

The Atkins Diet
Over the years the high-protein, low-carbohydrate diet has emerged from time to time. In each age, it has had a different name. Thirty years ago it was the Scarsdale Diet, or sometimes the Drinker's Diet. It is now back with us as the Atkins Diet, and for better or worse, it works.

The original Atkins diet, advertised by pictures of the late Dr Atkins brandishing the classic fry-up, has been abandoned. Even the Atkins machine now accepts that some carbohydrates are essential to human health, and that the proportion of saturated fat in the diet should be controlled. Yet its proponents still maintain that pure or nearly pure protein should be the basis of human diet – as it was, supposedly, in man's hunter-gatherer days. They maintain that, at that time, the meat eaten had little fat and that the carbohydrates all had a low glycaemic index – that is to say, the carbohydrate in rough seeds, beans and root vegetables was all unrefined and took time to absorb and metabolize. They don't include potatoes, with a high glycaemic index, nor, of course, modern bread.

When Dr Atkins died, his cardiovascular system was in poor order. His critics claim this was because he had eaten his unreformed, unmodified Atkins diet for too long. His advocates angrily deny this and claim that his tatty heart and his obesity were the results of incidental causes. Using an Atkins Diet to lose weight and to establish a lower calorie diet is, I think, justifiable – for a short time. Thereafter, however, it should be modified so that the calorie intake is kept down but a balanced diet is maintained.

Once the weight has been lost, no time should be wasted in starting the standard balanced diet. If a high-protein diet is to be pursued, total fats should not exceed 32 percent of the total calorie intake and only a small percentage should be saturated. It is usually taught that carbohydrates should form about 52 percent of the total calorie intake. A normal, healthy diet should be rich in fibre, provided you are not one of a sizeable minority of people whose gut problems are made worse by a high-fibre diet. Vitamins and trace elements are all-important.

Choosing the right diet

Just as no time can be lost before the dieter returns to a balanced diet so they should return to their childhood pattern of eating three meals a day without too many snacks. There is a difference between snacking and grazing. Grazers are those people who are able to have five or six small, balanced meals a day without overdoing it. Unfortunately, most of us are weak. Tell us to start grazing and we've denuded the grass from the pasture with our first meal and have continued to nibble for the rest of the day.

Choosing the right fruits

Five portions of vegetables or fruit are recommended by the governmental guidelines, and excellent advice it is, too – but this advice should be adapted to the needs of anyone seeking to lose weight. Many patients over the years have come to see me with stomachs that are straining their waistbands. They always assure me that they eat virtually no carbohydrates or sugar. It then transpires that they are drinking pints of orange juice daily, with grapefruit juice or other sugar-rich fruit juices every now and again for a change of flavour. They also supplement the fruit juices with bowls of fruit.

Many fruits are rich in highly refined sugars that are rapidly absorbed. A great load of fructose early in the day can have dramatic and undesirable effects on the body's metabolism, and furthermore the sugar in fruit is weight-increasing. A common piece of advice is to favour fruits grown in temperate climates rather than those imported from tropical ones; the former tend to have a lower glycaemic index. One school of thought suggests that the reason why fruits grown in a European temperate climate are better for weight loss is that if what sugars they contain are not so readily metabolized, there will not be such dramatic changes in the body's blood sugar. If blood-sugar levels can be evened out so that there is little variation during the day, then not only will the dieter be more apt to lose weight, he or she will not experience the crashing 'lows' produced by a drop in blood-sugar levels that often lead to cravings for the 'quick fix' of high-sugar, high-calorie junk foods.

On the vegetable front, the five-portions rule will contribute to providing the body's daily vitamin and mineral requirements. Yet the advice of nutritionalists who are able to grow their own vegetables in some pleasant university town and to bring their home-grown produce straight from the garden to the kitchen can be unrealistic. Most peoples' vegetables have travelled across England, Europe or the world before they are artificially ripened and reach the greengrocer or supermarket. Therefore, you might take a daily mineral and multivitamin tablet to fill in any deficiencies, as well as a fish oil capsule to ensure that even those who don't have two or three helpings of oily fish weekly will receive an adequate amount of essential fatty acids.

Organic food

There is much debate about the advantages or disadvantages of organic foods. There is no denying that fresh organic foods collected from the garden the morning they are cooked have a taste unlike any other vegetables and that their vitamin content is high. However, some evidence suggests, as much as it angers the organic farmers, that although there may be some improvement in the taste of organic vegetables, there is no real evidence that they are richer in any particular constituent.

Because so many vegetables, by the time they reach urban communities, have been harvested several days earlier, their vitamin content may well have been depleted – organic or not. Likewise, intensive agriculture has stripped many of the minerals out of the ground, and this is reflected in the mineral content of vegetables. I usually recommend that my patients, if they live in a city or if their vegetables have travelled further than they commute, should take a good-quality multivitamin and mineral supplement daily.

Other considerations

If possible, the healthy diet – whether you're trying to lose weight or simply to eat more healthily – should include fish, to provide the essential omega 3 fatty acids and vitamin D, as well as a couple of eggs a week. Coarse cereals are to be preferred to refined grains, and porridge has a better effect on the maintenance of a steady blood sugar than do most breakfast cereals. The manufacturers of breakfast cereals are becoming aware of this and are altering their ingredients accordingly.

Some potatoes are allowed in a well-balanced diet, but they should be boiled instead of baked or fried and, rather boringly, they should be old rather than new potatoes. This is because new potatoes have a high glycaemic index. Mashed potatoes, even without the butter, tend to be less good for the control of blood sugars and weight than elderly boiled potatoes.

Exercise as stress relief

Exercise – brisk, steady and regular – is an antedote to stress. The best exercises are those provided by brisk walking and cycling. Swimming is also a good exercise, provided that people know the conditions of their hearts. Doctors don't like to think about the number of patients they have had over the years who have died because they have dived into ice-cold water. However, if a person's heart is known to be in reasonable order and their blood pressure controlled, then swimming is an excellent exercise.

Even so, some caution must be observed. Older people or those with a family history of heart disease, diabetes, high blood pressure or any other condition that might have compromised the coronary circulation are well-advised to climb down slowly into the pool. Everyone knows that when they have a cold shower, there is an involuntary in-drawing of breath. This is because the autonomic nervous system has caused the smooth muscle in the air passages to constrict. At the instigation of cold, the coronary arteries may also behave like the air passages and contract. The result is that, for a moment, the blood supply to the heart muscle may be restricted, or the sudden changes in the heart circulation may cause a fatty plaque within the artery to rupture. In the worst-case scenario, the debris from it may block a narrowed artery and cause a coronary thrombosis.

Some people seek relaxation and relief from the troubles of the day by attending yoga or Pilates classes. Type A personalities, of course, may find all this a bit slow, and it is unlikely that when the yoga session reaches a stage of meditation they will be able to empty their minds enough to be only conscious of the sun or the noises of nature. Even so, yoga can be very useful as a form of stress-relief and control.

In contrast, violent exercise is never recommended. Running marathons or jogging may provide friends and fun, together with some funds for charity, but they are not life-lengthening. Likewise, that veteran rugby for the middle-aged is just an entertaining way of ensuring osteoarthritic joints ten years down the line. Once someone is too old for a competitive team sport, the best sort of exercise is to pursue an activity that will provide a social life and regular, steady exercise.

Walking

It's hard to beat brisk walking so far as exercise is concerned. The pace should be brisk enough to cause slight breathlessness, but not so strenuous that conversation, although difficult, becomes impossible. This type of walking will be sufficiently demanding to produce enough endorphins so that there will be a justifiably satisfying glow at the end of the walk. The walk should be not less than about half an hour a day. If a person's stress, genetic background or lifestyle (too much food and not enough exercise) has already led to metabolic diseases such as diabetes, the amount of exercise recommended is doubled.

People who for some reason don't want to walk can still bicycle. Some cardiologists who specialize in exercise physiology and its effect on the heart and health would dearly like to confine vigorous, but not strenuous, exercise to brisk walking and bicycling. Aside from stress considerations, in terms of healthy bones in both sexes, osteoporosis will only be inhibited when the limbs are bearing weight during exercise. Women should also remember that excessive exercise may also interfere with ovulation and menstruation and will actually favour the development of osteoporosis. Moderation in all things includes exercise. The objective of exercise must be movement.

*'Housework scares me. I'm writing a novel
to avoid getting started on it.'*

A word about gyms

Visits to the gym are now taking the place of team sports. The gym may not always be a rewarding choice for those who want to exercise non-competitively, but it never fails to provide satisfaction for people whose interest is studying human nature.

Gyms, however, are anything but relaxing. The members inevitably compete against each other. They start competing before they begin to exercise. They sum up each other's bodies and compare performances seven before they have begun their own routines. Even those men whose abdomens display six packs and whose biceps are bursting out of their T-shirts are boosting their own self-esteem by being unthinkingly critical of someone else's flab.

With red, sweating faces and a set expression, they struggle to burn up calories. There can't be an epidemiologist or endocrinologist who, when watching them, wouldn't worry about the effect of the stress hormones that must be pouring around their bodies. They have swapped the sweat shop of the computer room and a near-communal life in poorly separated 'pods' during the day for the sweat shop of the gym, with its mechanical gadgetry, outside working hours.

Tips for sensible, stress-busting exercising

1 Climb stairs; don't take lifts.

2 Walk or cycle to the local shops.

3 Plan household errands so as to ensure some walking.

4 Arrange to pick up an evening paper at some little distance from your house.

5 Garden. Gardening is much better exercise than most people realize.

6 Likewise, housework, especially hovering, is excellent exercise. One of the advantages of hoovering is the need to carry a fairly heavy machine up and down the stairs.

7 Walk not less than half an hour a day. People with early signs of metabolic disease or uncomplicated diabetes should double this to an hour.

8 If a person is a dog-lover, take the dog for long walks. These, too, should be brisk.

9 People with heart disease should not exercise briskly whenever the weather is too cold or if it is very humid. Extremes of temperature should be avoided.

10 As a form of exercise to keep Alzheimer's at bay or to prevent stress, exercise in which there is a social component is recommended.

Some exercises to relieve stress

Regardless of the stress a soldier feels on parade, if he allows his emotions to get the better of him and faints, the next stop is the guardroom. He is charged under Section 40 because, if only he had undertaken some simple muscular exercises (hidden by his uniform) while he waited on parade, his circulation would have remained tuned and he would never have ended up as an ignominious heap on the parade ground.

The army method of keeping the circulation flowing is to relax and tense the muscles of the legs, thighs and buttocks so that the blood is pumped back to the heart. Do this and you don't faint. As in the army, so in civilian life. There are some easy exercises you can do while sitting at your desk, travelling to work on the underground or sitting in a traffic jam. Some may save you from clogged arteries; others may help you to relax those aching, tense parts that betray the tension within you.

A series of exercises for those who don't believe, as I do, that forty minutes brisk walking a day is what is needed to keep healthy, are listed in various books. Despite its alternative title, the book *Joints and Glands Exercises* (see page 221), by Sri Swami Rama, provides a series of simple stretching exercises designed to increase circulation and decrease tension from the muscles and joints of the body. Some of these are listed on pages 205–208, with kind permission of the Himalayan Institute Press. They can be done in the office reasonably surreptitiously at any time of the day, and no one will think that the next managing director is about to desert Harley Street and the West End gym for an alternative lifestyle.

Forehead and sinus massage

All of these movements begin at the centre of the face and move outward. This pushes all the tension off the face, forehead and temples and smooths away any wrinkles on the forehead or crows-feet at the eye edges. This massage may also help break up and loosen mucus obstructions in the nasal sinuses.

•Sit in a comfortable posture with the head, neck and trunk straight. Make a loose fist with both hands, the thumbs against the forehead between the two eyebrows. Begin to massage the forehead with the thumbs by working up and out with a stroking motion. Follow the bony structure around the eyes and continue across the temples.

•Next, place the side of the thumbs on the face just below the eyes and next to the nose, one on each side. Make the same motions, moving outwards across the face and temples.

•Open the hands. Using the undersides of the thumbs, gently slide the thumbs across the upper rim of the eye sockets towards the temples.

•Likewise, massage with the index fingers the lower rim of the eye sockets towards the temples.

Eyes

Keep the head stationary and facial muscles relaxed in the following eye exercises. For several seconds after each variation, relax the eyes by gently closing them. All eye exercises can be done three times in each direction.

•Start with the eyes straight forward, then slowly turn them to the left as far as is comfortable. Feel the stretch in the eye muscles, then slowly come back to the forward position. Look to the right in the same manner, and again return to the forward position. Always balance what you do on one side by doing the same thing on the opposite side, holding the stretch for the same length of time in each direction.

•Turn the eyes towards the ceiling, then bring them back to the forward position. Look down, and again bring the eyes back to the forward position.

•Look to the upper left-hand corner of your eye socket. Bring the eyes back to the forward position. Look to the lower right-hand corner. Return the eyes to the forward position.

•Look at the lower left-hand corner; return to the forward position. Look towards the upper right-hand corner and again back to the forward position. Relax by closing the eyes.

•Look downward, then roll the eyes in a clockwise motion, making a complete circle. Reverse the process, moving the eyes in a counter-clockwise direction. Movement should be slow and free from jerks. Relax by closing the eyes.

•Close the eyes and squeeze the lids together tightly for five seconds. Now blink the eyelids as rapidly as you can. Relax by closing the eyes gently so the eyelids barely touch.

•Give the eyes a warmth-bath by rubbing the palms of the hands quickly together until the palms become hot, then gently lay them on the closed eyelids.

Neck

These exercises are very good for relieving accumulated tension in the back neck muscles. If you have tension headaches or are bothered by a stiff neck and shoulders, then these will be very helpful, and can be practised several times daily with ease.

Forward and backward bend Exhale slowly, bringing the head forward and taking the chin towards the chest. Feel the stretch of the muscles in the back of the neck. Inhale slowly, lifting the head up and back, stretching the muscles of the front of the neck. With an exhalation, slowly return to the forward position.

Chin over shoulder With an exhalation, turn the head as far to the left as possible and try to bring the chin in line with the shoulder. Inhale and bring the head back to the forward position. Repeat in the same manner on the right side.

Ear over shoulder With an exhalation, bring the left ear towards the left shoulder. Inhale and come back to the centre. Exhale and bring the right ear towards the right shoulder. Again, inhale, come back to the centre and relax. Only the head and neck should move. The shoulder should not be raised to meet the ear.

Turtle Keeping the shoulders stationary, exhale and thrust the chin and head as far forward as comfortable, keeping the mouth closed and the teeth together. Inhaling, slowly come back to the centre; then moving the head back, tuck the chin into the neck, forcing an extreme double chin. Exhale and relax, returning to the centre position.

Neck rolls Lower the chin to the chest and slowly begin to rotate the head in a clockwise direction. Inhale while lifting the head up and back, and exhale when bringing it forward and down. Reverse and rotate the same number of times in the opposite, counter-clockwise direction. The head, neck and body should be relaxed, allowing the head to rotate freely and loosely.

Lion posture While sitting in a chair, lean forward. Throw the shoulders forward, exhale and thrust the chin and head as far forward as comfortable, opening the mouth wide and thrusting the tongue out and down, trying to touch the chin. At the same time, place hands on the knees, arms straight, with fingers widely spread, exerting a pull on hands, arms and shoulders. They eyes should be focused on the point between the two eyebrows. The whole body should be stretched. Hold the breath while briefly holding this position. Sit back and relax with an inhalation, and repeat.

Shoulders
Stand or sit with the arms hanging loosely at the sides. Begin to rotate the left shoulder in a complete circle, first moving it forward and in towards the centre of the chest, exhaling as you do. Then move it up towards the ear and back while inhaling, trying to touch the shoulder-blade to the spine, and then down back into the starting position. Rotate three times in this direction and then reverse and rotate three times in the opposite direction. Do the same for the right shoulder, and then do both shoulders together. Relax.

Relaxation exercises

I was never an enthusiast for yoga until I sampled it briefly on a trip to study Indian medicine. Now I am sufficiently won over to recommend a few simple yoga-type exercises that should help people relax.

The following stretches and relaxation exercises are taken from *Hatha Yoga Manual I* by Samskrti and Veda (see bibliography, page 221), and reprinted with the kind permission of the Himalayan Institute Press. They provide a good basic introduction to hatha yoga postures. The manual advises nine rules that should be followed when undertaking the exercises.

1 Set a specific time each day for practice. This should be when you are not rushed. Practise at least a little every day.

2 Morning and evening are the two best times to practise. Morning exercise helps you remain calm and alert during the day. In the evening, the exercises help relieve the day's tensions so that you can enjoy a peaceful night's sleep.

3 Do the exercises in a clean, quiet and well-ventilated room. Wear loose, comfortable clothing.

4 Always practise on an empty stomach.

5 Women should not practise strenuous exercises during menstruation.

6 Do not become discouraged if your body does not respond the same way each day. Just keep practising regularly and don't compete with others.

7 Study your body and its movements. Be aware of your capacity and don't go beyond it. It will increase in time.

8 Let the body movements flow evenly and gently with the breath. Don't hold your breath at any time unless instructed.

9 Follow any exertion with relaxation. However, do not allow the mind to drift toward sleep while you relax.

Sun salutation

When asleep, the body is at its most inactive. During this time, the conscious mind goes 'off-line' and the metabolism decreases; circulation slows and all other bodily functions are considerably reduced. Upon waking, both body and mind must make a transition from this inactive condition to one of activity. The smoother this transition, the less chance of stress.

The sun salutation aids in this transition by massaging and stimulating crucial parts of the body, including the glands, organs, muscles and nerves. The breathing rate increases, bringing more oxygen into the lungs. This increases the heart rate, which in turn causes more blood to pass through the lungs, where it picks up oxygen, and thus sends a greater supply of oxygenated blood throughout the body.

The sun salutation is made up of twelve positions. Each should flow into the next in one graceful, continuous movement. When attempting the salutation for the first time, read through and become familiar with all the movements, and then practise coordinating the breath with them. This exercise is designed to stretch and limber the spine as well as all of the joints and limb: the perfect antidote to a stressful day. All exercise instructions on pages 211–215 are taken from *Hatha Yoga Manual I*.

Position One (exhaling during movement)
Stand firmly with the head, neck and trunk in a straight line. Beginners can stand with the feet slightly apart. With palms together in prayer position, place the hands before the heart and gently close the eyes. Standing silently, concentrating on the breath.

Position Two (inhaling during movement)
Inhaling, slightly lower and stretch the hands and arms forward with the palms facing downward. Raise the arms overhead until they are next to the ears. Keeping the legs straight and the head between the arms, arch the spine and bend backward as far as possible without straining.

Position Three (exhaling during movement)
Exhaling, bend forward from the hips, keeping the back straight and the arms next to the ears. Continue bending; place the palms next to the feet, aligning the fingers with the toes. Bring the head to the knees, keeping the legs straight. Note: if you cannot place the hands on the floor without bending the legs, then lower only as far as comfortable without straining.

Position Four (inhaling during movement)
In this position, bend the knees, if necessary, in order to place the hands on the floor. Inhaling, stretch the right leg back, rest the right knee and the top of the right foot on the floor, and extend the toes. The left foot remains between the hands; the hands remain firmly on the floor. Arch the back, look up, and stretch the head back as far as comfortable. The line from the head to the tip of the right foot should form a smooth and graceful curve.

Position Five (briefly holding the breath)

Curl the toes of the right foot and extend the left leg, placing it next to the right. The arms remain straight and the body forms an inclined plane from the head to the feet. This position resembles a starting push-up position.

Position Six (exhaling during movement)

Exhaling, drop first the knees, and then the chest to the floor, keeping the tips of the fingers in line with the breasts. Tuck in the chin and place the forehead on the floor. In this position, only the toes, knees, hands, chest and forehead touch the floor. The nose does not touch the floor and the elbows remain close to the body.

Position Seven (inhaling during movement)

Without moving the hands and forehead, relax the legs and extend the feet so that the body rests flat on the floor. Inhaling, slowly raise the head. First, touch the nose and then the chin to the floor; then stretch the head forward and upward. Without using the strength of the arms or hands, slowly raise the shoulders and chest; look up and bend back as far as is comfortable. In this posture the navel remains on the floor. To lift the thorax, use the muscles of the back only. Do not use the arms and hands to push the body off the floor, but to balance the body. Keep the feet and legs together and relaxed.

Position Eight (exhaling during movement)

Without repositioning the feet and hands, straighten the feet so that they point towards the hands. Exhaling, straighten the arms and push the buttocks high in the air. Bring the head between the arms and try to press the heels gently to the floor.

Position Nine (inhaling during movement)

Inhaling, bend the right knee and place the right foot between the hands. Align the toes with the fingers. Rest the left knee and the top of the foot on the floor and extend the toes. Arch the back, look up, and bend back as far as is comfortable.

Position Ten (exhaling during movement)

Exhaling, place the left foot beside the right foot, keeping the palms on the floor. Straighten the legs and bring the head to the knees.

Position Eleven (inhaling during movement)

Inhaling, slowly raise the body, stretching the arms out, up and back. Remember to keep the arms next to the ears and to keep the legs straight.

Position Twelve (exhaling)

Exhaling, return to an erect standing position. Slowly lower the arms and bring the hands to the chest in prayer position. Repeat the sun salutation, but alternate the leg movements by extending the opposite leg in positions four and nine; then relax.

Other stretch and relaxation exercises

Side stretch

Assume a simple standing posture. Begin inhaling, and slowly raise the right arm out to the side, with the palm facing downward. When the arm reaches shoulder level, turn the palm upward. Continue inhaling and raise the arm until it is next to the ear. Still continuing to inhale and keeping the feet firmly on the floor, stretch the entire right side of the body upward. Then, without allowing the body to bend forward or backward or the right arm to bend, begin exhaling and slowly bend at the waist, sliding the left hand down the left leg. Breathe evenly for three complete breaths. Inhaling, slowly bring the body back to an upright position. Exhaling, lower the arm slowly to shoulder level, turn the palm downward, and return to the simple standing posture. Concentrate on the breath until the body relaxes completely. Repeat the side stretch in the opposite direction.

Simple back stretch

Assume the standing posture. With the fingers facing downward, place the heels of the hands on either side of the spine just above the buttocks. Exhaling, gently push the hips forward, slowly letting the head, neck and trunk bend backward as far as comfortable without straining. Inhaling, return to the standing pose, keeping the hands in the same position. Keeping the entire body relaxed, slowly bend the body forward as far as possible. Hold this position until all the muscles of the back relax.

Angle posture

Assume the simple standing posture with the feet two to three feet apart. Placing the arms behind the back, grasp the right wrist with the left hand. Keep the heels in line and place the right foot at a ninety-degree angle from the left. Inhaling, turn the body toward the right foot. Exhaling, bend forward from the hips and bring the head as close to the knee as comfortable. Breathe evenly; hold this position for five counts. Inhaling, slowly raise the body; exhaling, turn to the front. Turn the right foot so that it faces forward. Repeat the exercise on the left side.

Second Position

Keeping the arms straight, interlace the fingers behind the back. With the right foot at a ninety-degree angle from the left, turn the body and bend forward from the hips, bringing the head toward the right knee. Raise the hands overhead as far as comfortable. Breathe evenly; hold this position for five counts. Inhaling, slowly raise the body and turn to the front. Repeat this exercise on the left side. Repeat the exercise to the front, with both feet facing forward.

Third Position

With the arms straight, interlace the fingers behind the back and press the palms together. Exhaling, raise the arms and bend forward as far as comfortable. Breathe evenly and hold for five counts. Inhaling, push the hands toward the floor and bend the head, neck and trunk back as far as comfortable without straining. Breathe evenly; hold for five counts. Slowly return to a standing position and relax.

Useful contacts

Alcohol-related problems
Alcoholics Anonymous
+44 (0) 1904 644026

Al-Anon and Alateen (for families)
+44 (0) 141 339 8884

Children
Family Service Units
+44 (0) 207 402 5175

Parentline
+44 (0) 207 284 5500
Helpline: +44 (0)808 8002222

Counselling
British Association of Counselling
+44 (0) 1788 550899

British Association of Psychotherapists
+44 (0) 208 452 9823

Careline (confidential counselling on any issue)
+44 (0) 208 514 1177

The National Council of Psychotherapists
+44 (0)845 2306072

Death and bereavement
Cruse Bereavement Care
+44 (0) 208 940 4818

Depression
MIND (National Association for Mental Health)
Infoline: +44 (0) 845 7660163

Depression Alliance
+44 (0) 207 633 9929
Scotland: +44 (0) 131 467 3050
Wales:+44 (0) 1222 521774

Divorce
National Council for One-Parent Families
UK only: 0800 0185026

National Council for the Divorced & Separated
+44 (0) 7041 478120

Eating Disorders
Eating Disorders Association
Helpline:+44 (0) 1603 621414

National Centre for Eating Disorders
+44 (0) 1372 469493

Financial problems
Citizens Advice Bureau
+44 (0) 208 684 2236

Menopause
The Amarant Trust (menopause and HRT)
Adviceline: +44 (0) 207 793 9980

Miscarriage
The Miscarriage Association
+44 (0) 10924 200799

Parents
Carers National Association
+44 (0) 1695 735420

Panic Attacks and Phobias
Fear of Flying
+44 (0) 870 3500767

HOPE (Help Overcome Panic Effects)
 +44 (0) 207 729 9418

No Panic
Helpline: +44 (0) 1952 590545

National Phobics Society
+44 (0) 870 770 0456

PAX (Panic Attacks and Anxiety)
+44 (0) 207 468 2116

Pregnancy
Family Planning Association
+44 (0) 845 3101334

Foresight Association
+44 (0) 1483 427839

Relationships and Sexual problems
Relate
+44 (0) 1788 573241

Brook Advisory Centres (advice on sexual problems)
UK only: 0800 0185023

The Sexual Dysfunction Association
Helpline: +44 (0) 870 7743571

Retirement
Age Concern
+44 (0) 208 765 7200
Info line, UK only: 0800 009966

Stress Management
Impact Factory
+44 (0) 207 226 1877

Suicide
The Samaritans
+44 (0) 845 7909090

Yoga
British Wheel of Yoga
+44 (0) 1529 306851

Select bibliography

Benson, Herbert. *The Relaxation Response*. London: William Collins Sons & Co Ltd, 1977.

Charlton, Bruce. *Psychiatry and the Human Condition*. Abingdon, Oxfordshire, England: Radcliffe Medical Press Ltd, 2000.

Dunitz, Martin. *Generalized Anxiety Disorder: Diagnosis, Treatment and its Relationship to Other Anxiety Disorders*. London: Martin Dunitz Ltd, 1988.

Gill, Jit. *Stress Survival Guide*. London: HarperCollins, 1999.

Hanson, Peter. *The Joy of Stress*. London: Pan Books Ltd, 1986.

Herbert, Claudia, and Wetmore, Ann. *Overcoming Traumatic Stress: a Self-help Guide using Cognitive Behavioural Techniques*. London: Robinson Publishing Ltd, 1999.

Holmes, Thomas, and Rahe, Richard. 'Social Readjustment Rating Scale'. The version in this book is adapted and reprinted from *Journal of Psychosomatic Research*, volume II, Thomas Holmes and Richard Rahe, 'Social Readjustment Rating Scale', p. 214, 1967, with permission from Elsevier Inc.

Livingston Booth, Audrey. *Stressmanship*. London: Severn House Publishers Ltd, 1985.

Locker, Terry, and Gregson, Olga. *Stresswise: a Practical Guide for Dealing with Stress*. London: Hodder & Stoughton, 1989.

Nuernberger, Phil. *Freedom from Stress*. Honesdale, Pennsylvania: Himalayan Institute Press, 1981.

Rama, Sri Swami.(Ballentine, Rudolph M, MD Ed.) *Joints and Glands Exercises as Taught By Sri Swami Rama of the Himalayas*. Honesdale, Pennsylvania. Himalayan Institute Press, 1977.

Rowe, Dorothy. *Depression: the Way out of Your Prison*. London: Routledge and Kegan Paul, 1996.

Samskrti and Veda. *Hatha Yoga Manual I*. Honesdale, Pennsylvania: Himalayan Institute Press, 1977.

Shealy, C Norman, MD. *Ninety Days to Stress-Free Living: a Day-by-Day Health Plan Including Exercises, Diet and Relaxation Techniques*. Dorset, England: Element Books Ltd, 1999.

Index

About the author

Dr Tom Stuttaford was born in Norfolk. He has won a popular following for his writing on all aspects of health and medical matters in *The Times*. His previous published works include *What's Up, Doc? Understanding Your Common Symptoms*, published by Little Books, and *To Your Good Health* and *In Your Right Mind*, published by Faber & Faber, in addition to *The Harvard Medical Encyclopedia*, published by Cassell. Tom divides his time between London and Norwich.